To

My Dearest John

lots of love

Dan xx

I knew you would love this

X

THE BOOK OF
BRAUNTON

AVRIL STONE

HALSGROVE

TO JEANIE

My dearest friend and mentor

Title page: *Vellator in the early twentieth century*

First published in Great Britain in 2014

Copyright © Avril Stone

British Library Cataloguing-in-Publication Data
A CIP record for this title is available from the British Library

ISBN 978 0 85704 238 5

HALSGROVE
Halsgrove House,
Ryelands Business Park,
Bagley Road, Wellington, Somerset TA21 9PZ
Tel: 01823 653777   Fax: 01823 216796
email: sales@halsgrove.com

Part of the Halsgrove group of companies.
Information on all Halsgrove titles is available at: www.halsgrove.com

Printed and bound in the UK by TJ International Ltd

CONTENTS

Acknowledgements

After an eight year adventure to the west coast of Scotland with my husband Eric we returned to our 'Ain Folk' in North Devon and I kept the promise I made ten years ago to write the *Book of Braunton.*

Like many people who visit Braunton regularly I thought I knew the village quite well. However, once I began my research it became obvious to me there was a fascinating history of seafaring, farming and the memories of the people who had lived, worked and socialised here over the past century.

These community history books can only work with the co-operation and willingness of the community to share their memories with you. Over the last two years I have been most grateful to all those who did just that and for the hours they spent telling me their stories as well as allowing me to use their photographs all 748 of them!

During the time covered by this book it was usual for local photographers to attend carnivals, fêtes and shows to record the events of the day. (These images could then be purchased at a later date and sometimes they would be published in the local newspaper.) Many of the photographs given to me for this book had to be scanned from the owner's albums and scrapbooks and so it was not possible to see if there was a photographer's name was on the reverse of the picture. I therefore apologise if some photographers have not had their work acknowledged.

It must be appreciated that everyone remembers an occasion differently and the events in this book may be different from how you remember them. It does not mean that either is wrong but displays how your memory of an occasion is unique to you.

With respect to the older generation who have reminded me throughout the last two years that I must use the correct spelling I have used two L's in Vellator. I hope this doesn't cause too much disagreement!

For all their constant help and support my special thanks go to my husband Eric and my dear friend Jean Woodhams and her trusted red subbing pen – I don't know what I'd do without both of them.

Special thanks also to Bill Mitchell and Tom Welch for teaching me so much about seafaring that I'm sure I could fill another book with all the shipping terms and knowledge. Thanks also to Jane Fewings and the volunteers of the Braunton Museum for allowing me to use the Museum to interview people.

Please excuse any mistakes in names or details as there are bound to be some but I have checked and double checked where I can.

Once again I am most grateful to all who have contributed to this book. Their names are listed below in alphabetical order:

Marilyn Abbott, Marie Ash, John Avery, Julian Avery, Nancy Barnes, Denzil Bath, Albert Beer, Christine Braund, Michael Butler, Eddie Chichester, Elaine Christie, John Clarke, Brian and Jean Clarke, Maurice Clements, Professor Jean Crabtree, Sue Cresswell, Thelma Crook, Shirley Curtis, Barbara Dadds, Simon Daukes, Dorothy Davies, Margaret Dent, Roland Dibble, Rita Drayton, Margaret Dudley, Elizabeth Dyer, Christine Dymond, Hilary Edmonds, Brian Ellis, John Fry, David Fry, Andy Ford, John Hall, Kathleen Harris, Robert Harris, John and Jane Hartnoll, Lorna Henderson, Don Hill, Joy Hill, Gillian Hoskins, Keith Howes, Mervyn and Monica Huxtable, Joan Incledon, Lorraine Irwin, Graham Jenkins, Clare Keast, James Leonard, -Rev. Robert Manning, Mike Marshall, Steve Massie, Paul and Rosemary Madgett, Andy Martin, Ross Moon, Pam Munt, George and Jillian Legge, Judy Nolan of Braunton Academy, Brian Norman, John Phillips, Phil Powell, Barbara Price, John Prior, Richard Prior, Dougie Reed, Tony Reed, Poppy Richards, Eileen Salter, Wendy Saunders, Ian Scott, Alison Serret, Amanda Skinner, Nancy Skinner, Les Smith, 'Smudge' Smith, Bob Thatcher, Irene and Cyril Therin, Rev. Anne Thorne, Jean Tilke, Jean Traill, Norman Venner, Ruth Watts, Christine Watts, Tracey Weaver – Clerk to the Parish Council, Brian Williams, Neil Worth of Kingfisher Multimedia and Geraldine Wright.

I must also mention the sad loss this year of a good friend, Steve Knight who has always been most generous in allowing me the use of his grandfather's photographs for my books. There are very few homes and businesses in Devon that do not have an R. L. Knight print on their walls. The historical information in these photographs of our towns, villages and local events is invaluable.

And last but by no means least my thanks go to my publishers Halsgrove for their help and expertise, with a special mention for Steven, Denise, Karen and Sharon.

Foreword

Braunton the Big Village with a Big Heart – one of the oldest villages in the kingdom with its origins in farming and seafaring. A village which once had as many as 20 farms within its streets and still has great pride in preserving one of England's only two 'open strip' field systems – The Great Field. A village that is a gateway to the golden sands of North Devon.

This is not your usual history book although it goes back to ancient times it is mostly the personal memories of people who have lived, worked, been schooled or associated in any way with this vibrant, Devonshire community.

Whilst researching I was made only too aware that time is running out to gather the living history of the people of the twentieth century, when four or five of long lived residents of Braunton died within weeks of each other. And with them died their memories.

Congratulations to the Braunton Museum and its band of volunteers who with great pride have worked so hard to capture the life and times of their village and its people with publications and artefacts. It may only be a small building but it holds a wealth of knowledge which should not be missed.

Here are stories of the seafaring, farming and railways. Of wartime, when the RAF operated from Chivenor (and remained in the hearts of people ever since) and of course when the American Army made the village their tented base for a while. Schooling, the many trades within its streets, religious life, carnivals, emergency services, sporting clubs and life in today's Braunton are captured in this book which records the past for the present and future to enjoy.

Score Bridge close to the railway crossing linking Station Road to Chapel Street. Circa 1920.

The Square, Braunton. The heart of the village was the old Cross Tree where the coaches and later the buses stopped, carnivals and public events held and the town crier made his announcements. And of course children played and adults caught up with the latest news.

South Street in the 1920s.

Chapter 1

Times Past

Once upon a time it is written that a Welsh missionary travelled across the sea and found a settlement haven on the sheltered shores of North Devon. Here he converted the inhabitants to Christianity and built a church which is named after him – St Brannock's.

It was in the sixth century and the inhabitants mainly survived by the diverse use of farm land and the sea. St Brannock settled in the village which became Braunton.

There has been a settlement at Braunton for more than a thousand years as it is ideally geographically placed, with hills to the north for protection from the winds and the River Caen running through into the Taw and Torridge estuary. There was also, rich alluvial soil of the Great Field and marshes for farming.

Braunton's importance was noted in the Domesday Book of 1086 when, like its close neighbour Barnstaple, it was a royal manor. In time Barnstaple expanded into the major manufacturing, ship-building and commercial borough whereas Braunton continued as a mainly agricultural and seafaring community.

Until the railway was built in 1874 there were two main roads into and out of the village – heading north from Barnstaple and south from Ilfracombe to their junction on the Square with its old tree where folk gathered to chat.

When you are aware of the width of these roads you have to wonder how it was possible for vehicles to pass each other. When a waggoner was asked how he would pass another in Church Street, he replied that he didn't! He would stop at the top or bottom of the street and listen. If he could hear the jangling of the horse trappings he knew something was travelling along the road so he would wait until it passed him.

At the bottom of Church Street the London coach would stop at the New Inn to change horses and for the passengers to enjoy a meal before the last stretch of their journey to Ilfracombe. East and Church Streets were the main shopping and business thoroughfares. South Street was the road to Vellator and to the seagoing vessels; so many seafarers lived in this street. Caen Street, named after the river that runs through the village, goes to the beautiful beaches and villages of Saunton, Croyde, Putsborough and Georgeham.

The opening of Chaloners Road in 1924. (The new road between Ilfracombe and Braunton). L to R: Unknown, Sgt Hutchings, unknown, Charles West, Sidney Hartnoll, Capt. Incledon-Webber, Robert Perryman, George Frankpitt, unknown, John Passmor, John Tucker (Saunton), William Easton and William Isaac.

When the railway arrived and the new main Ilfracombe to Barnstaple road was cut through the centre of the village between 1924 and 1931 the Braunton area opened up to holiday-makers, and all the business enterprises that go along with this – hotels, B&Bs, shops, taxi and car hire and, of course, the beaches and subsequently the sport of surfing the waves!

The railway also opened up travelling further afield to work and of sending perishable goods long distances. Milk, cream, flowers, fish and rabbits were now sent overnight to many places – mainly London

The new prosperity saw the village expand from the close-knit country unit to a commuter and retirement housing area and one which in the holiday season becomes one of North Devon's most popular holiday centres.

Opening of the Parish Hall in 1926.

The crowds wait outside the newly built George Hotel for the tape to be cut and the new Exeter Road to be opened in 1931.

Left: *Felling the Cross Tree in the Square in February, 1935.*

Below: *The tree had to be removed due to the increasing traffic.*

Chapter 2

The Great Field and Marshes

View from West Hill over the Great Field, marshes and the Taw and Torridge Estuary.

For a breath-taking view climb to the top of West Hill or East Hill on a clear day and soak up the magnificence of the Taw and Torridge Estuary and the towns and villages that abound. Below you is Braunton with its unique agricultural system – the Great Field that dates back to medieval times and is one of only two remaining in England today.

The Great Field, Braunton Marshes and Horsey Island together amount to 2000 acres. The River Caen flows through the village and along the eastern boundary of the marshes before joining the tidal Taw Estuary at Vellator. This river plays an important part in the maintenance of life on the marshes.

The Great Field itself extends to 350 acres and is a classic example of the medieval, communal agricultural system used throughout the country where work and tools were shared.

In the first instance there were two great areas of field. One was tilled with crops and the other left fallow to graze the cattle.

Later they became just the one field which was divided into long narrow strips. Each strip measured a chain (22 yards) in width and a furlong (220 yards) in length. This was the amount of land it was thought an oxen could plough in one day. (In the Domesday Book of 1086 it is noted that Braunton had 30 ploughs.)

John Hartnoll sowing potatoes in the Great Field.

Each strip was separated by a grass-covered ridge known as a baulk, the ends marked by 'bond stones' which were large pebbles from the beach.

The parish priest allocated the strips of land to each family every year.

A 'three strip' system was used – one for wheat or rye for bread making, one for barley to produce beer (beer was safer to drink that water) and the third was left fallow. Each year the crops were moved to the next strip leaving one to rest and revive.

In 1905 there were around 490 strips of land under cultivation – by 60 farmers. In 1982 there were only five farmers working the field. The same is true today. There are more owners of the land but some of these do not use it themselves but rent it to those five farmers who work together and rotate their crops yearly. Although the thousand year old practice of Brauntonians communally providing for themselves diminished long ago, the ethos is still alive.

Braunton Marshes

South of the Great Field lies Braunton Marsh which, up to the nineteenth century was used for grazing the parish live-stock. However, every time there was a high tide these animals had to be moved as the sea flooded over the marsh.

It was decided to construct a sea wall to keep the tide out as well as lay a drainage system throughout the entire marshland.

Between 1812 and 1815 work on enclos-ing the land and draining the marshes took place and as there was not enough local labour, workmen were imported from Cornwall, Ireland and Holland. Drainage canals were built on three sides of the marsh and a 3 mile embankment was built from Vellator to Broadsands with a footpath along the whole length of it. A rough road ran along the inner side of the bank with a closed gate which kept the animals from straying. A house was built for a marsh inspector (today's Toll House). Further improve-ments over the years were straightening the Pill to allow larger vessels to come further up the river, where they also built a new quay at Vellator.

There came a great south westerly gale force storm causing disastrous damage to this sea wall on 16 December 1910. With a high tide and violent winds the wall was breached and Horsey Island marsh flooded, drowning many of the stock.

James Darracott Reed, whose father Claude farmed at Manor Farm, Wrafton was only five years old in 1910 and his memories of this fatal event were

The sea bank on Horsey Island is breached during the great storm on the 16 December, 1910.

The farmers survey the devastation of all their lost animals after the flood receded.

recorded on a C.D. which was given to me by James's grandson Tony Reed.

James recalled that his father had gone to Barnstaple Market and the weather became so bad that their mother came to meet him and his brother from school with the horse and trap.

They got to within half a mile of the farmhouse when the howling wind brought three trees down, "just like nine pins". The pony reared and the trap went over, throwing them all out. The pony was caught under a tree. Mother and the boys struggled back home and a farmhand was sent back to free the pony.

Claude at the Cattle Market was approached by three sailors who told him how bad the sea was when they had come in over the Bar.

They knew he had animals grazing out on the marshes and they thought these animals were in danger due to the freak weather conditions. In fact there were 20 head of cattle, two horses and 200 head of sheep grazing out on the marshes. ('Salt grass is the best for flavouring mutton,' James tells us.)

His father dashed home and changed horses then galloped 3 miles to the marshes where the gale was still howling. He rounded up the cart colts and the cattle and then went back to round up the sheep, but in an instant the bank burst and the sea came through and all the sheep were drowned.

Rabbits were blamed for the demise of the sea bank as it was said that so many of them had burrowed into one side of the bank that it had weakened it. Amazingly some rabbits were found alive at the tops of trees where they had sought refuge from the flood water.

It was a very difficult job to rebuild and extra labour had to be imported. Every time the breached area was filled the next tide washed away all the work that had been done. Eventually two old ketches were sunk and filled with stones and this seemed to work. Other methods were also used, some proved useless and others were successful. It took three years to rebuild the sea bank.

Braunton Marshes
Internal Drainage Board

Roland Dibble of Warren Farm, Saunton, has been involved with the marshes since he first started work at the farm when he left school at the age of fourteen. He had moved in with the Packer family in 1942. In 1957 Roland took on the tenancy from Christie Estates.

There are seven elected landowners on the Drainage Board. Three of these are Marsh Inspectors and Roland is one of these and responsible for the water levels in the drainage dykes. If there are any complaints that one of the owners hasn't any water on his land Roland has to sort out the problem.

Every land owner pays drainage rates and their land is rated regarding the quality of the fields, as some are better than others. These rates pay for the water and the maintenance of the dykes.

One warm sunny spring day Roland took me around the marshes and explained that the water system worked mainly by gravity with a slight incline of the land. A spring to the north of the marshes brings fresh water into the system and it must be kept moving to keep it aerated. In hot, dry weather, in order to keep the water levels up in the dykes, fresh water can be taken from the River Caen at Vellator Bridge and Roland controls the amount of water diverted into the system.

With water constantly entering the dykes it has to have an exit and the only place you can let it out is at the Great Sluice beside the Toll Road onto Horsey Island. This system is the same as when it was installed 200 years ago – simple but efficient. Two

Marsh Inspector, Roland Dibble regulates the amount of water that flows from the River Caen into Braunton Marshes.

Roland Dibble altering the water level in the dykes on the marsh.

The tidal gates of the Great Sluice that close when the tide comes in, to prevent salt water entering the dykes. They open on their own when the tide goes out to allow fresh water to leave the marshes.

great wooden gates open and shut with the tide. When the tide comes in the gates shut to keep the salt water from entering the marsh dykes and when the tide goes out the gates open again and the fresh water from the marshes can be released.

Dykes are in the place of hedges as well as being a supply of fresh water for the sheep and cattle. Roland told me that cattle and sheep that are reared on the marshes produce the very best beef and lamb for the table.

The Drainage Board meet regularly throughout the year and

discuss the condition of the dykes and decide which ones need to be cleared of weed. This is a very delicate job as the base of each dyke is lined with clay and if this is damaged all the water in the system would drain away. Years ago this work would have been done by several workmen; today it is one man and a digger but a digger operated with the greatest of care! Other responsibilities of the board are the upkeep of the toll road, sea bank and the car parks. This is where your money goes when you pay at the Toll House to travel to Crow Point.

The Toll House was built as a rent free house for an employee of the Marsh Inspectors and for this free accommodation they were expected to check on the water levels in the dykes, clear the drains and cut the weeds. They also had to control the wildlife that may burrow into the sea bank and weaken it. They would also get paid by the farmers to tend their stock and of course take the tolls from everyone using the road.

Now half way through his seventh decade and with the vast majority of those years spent tending to the Braunton Marshes, Roland says it's been a good life. He and his wife Jo mostly enjoy watching all the wildlife – the herons, egrets, dip-chicks and swans. He recalled the day they saw a badger run across the field from a swan's nest. They found the eggs had been pulled out of the nest, so rescued them and put them back. They watched as the swan came back, sat on the eggs and sometime later hatched them all.

That's what I call job satisfaction!

Brian Clarke who lives at Down Lane can look down on the Toll House – which he calls Bank House – where his mother Elizabeth was born and grew up.

Simon Drayton, the Toll House Keeper collecting the fee to drive to Crow Point.

Elizabeth Williams marries Arthur Clarke from her home at the Toll House in 1930.

Chapter 3

A Village of Farms

If you know the older part of Braunton as it is today can you imagine what it was like to have 19 working farms in these tightly built streets! Very few had any fields in close proximity. There were just the farmhouse, yard and barns and maybe an orchard. This meant the cattle had to be put out to grass in the fields outside the village or on Braunton Marsh and the milking cows brought home through the village streets twice a day.

Nancy Barnes who lives at North Buckland has vivid memories of her life as a young girl in Braunton. Born at Broadgate Farm in East Street in March 1918 with her twin sister Minnie they were the daughters of Bert and Evalyn (always known as Minnie) Lane.

Bert Lane was the youngest of William and Eliza Lane's nine children and ran the farm with his parents although Nancy says it was her grandmother Eliza who was the business head of the family. William died in 1903 and in 1910 Eliza bought the farm from the Williams estate when they were left

Nancy Barnes' family. Back row: *Her father Albert Lane and a cousin of her mother's Mr Tucker. In the front: twins Nancy and Minnie, baby brother William, her mother Evalyn (also known as Minnie) and elder sister Grace.*

The Lane Family of Broadgate Farm in 1902. (Written on the back of the photograph by Nancy Barnes) L to R: Aunts Florrie Gould, Vin Hernaman, Jessie Perryman, Grandfather William Lane and Grandmother Eliza Lane née Pugsley, Uncle William Lane and his only son Philip and Albert Lane (the youngest in the family and Nancy's father). Grandfather William died in 1903.

with crippling expenses to repair the damage after the great flood of Horsey Bank.

Before Chaloner's Road was built in 1924 the land behind Broadgate Farm went right down to the River Caen. Nancy says that there was an orchard almost all the way to the river where she would play with her sisters and sometimes paddle their feet. The family used to sell their produce from the farmhouse – milk, fruit, vegetables and poultry.

Nancy, Grace and Minnie at Broadgate Farm in 1931.

"Things began to change when we were fourteen years old, as the milk carts started coming in. These were a horse and trap with two large cans, one with fresh milk and one with skimmed. The skimmed had the cream taken off the top and was cheaper, and so people bought it for making puddings".

In 2009, when Nancy recorded her memories of her young life, she could name nineteen farms actually in the streets of Braunton – Steppes Farm in Silver Street and Chapple Hill Farm on Chapple Hill, Broadgate; Myrtle and Mock Farms in East Street and Caen Farm in that street. In North Street there were six farms – Town, Gordon's, The Staddon's, Brindles, Skur and another where the Atkins were the famers. Chapple Street had five farms – West Cross Farm (later known just as Cross Farm) and Score Farm and three farms owned by W. Sussex and E. Sussex and another by Mr Delbridge. This leaves two farms in South Street, one owned by William Palmer and the other owned by her grandfather William Lane's family, South Street Farm. Today there are no farms in the village.

As you have read in the previous chapter, many farmers had parcels of land of varying sizes on the Great Field where the cereals, crops and vegetables were grown.

Nancy's parents Bert and Minnie died in 1940. The farm was taken over by their only son William who was about to marry Doris Friend. Nancy's elder sister Grace later became a farmer's wife when she married Richard Welch of Buckland Farm and Nancy also married farmer Tom Barnes of North Buckland. To read that story you must turn to Chapter Seven.

Another village farm without any surrounding fields was Town Farm in North Street in the ownership of the Hartnoll family for generations. I met with John and Jane Hartnoll and their son David who now own Broadlands Farm on the edge of the Great Field where they are one of the five farms who work the Great Field today.

Nancy celebrates her ninety-fifth birthday in 2013.

John's Great Grandfather George Perryman Hartnoll owned a large amount of land in the Great Field and like John was a Marsh Inspector. George's son William and his wife Florence had six sons and three daughters and they took over the farm when George died in 1909 at the age of ninety-four.

All six sons worked on the land at some time in their lives. Fred and Jim went to Canada to farm. George had land on Braunton Down that looked out to sea. As he watched the ketches coming and going through Barnstaple Bay he realised he had a calling for the sea. He eventually became the Master of the vessel *Eilian* and traded from Vellator. He married May Newcombe who was a stewardess on the vessel. He retired as Master of the *Eilian* in 1934 and with May moved to Teignmouth and became a senior pilot for Trinity House.

Leonard worked for Lake's Bakery in Caen Street. He was a big chap and in the early years of WWI when he was only seventeen he lied about his age and signed up for the army and went to war in France. He was taken as a P. O. W. for the last three years of the war. When he returned home to the farm it was obvious to his family and friends that he was suffering from severe shell shock which remained with him for the rest of his life. He was a gentle giant of a man who was content to help his brother Ernest on the farm and

The Hartnoll family at Town Farm. L-R: Leonard, John with daughter Jill, Ernest and John's son David.

later his nephew John. Jane said when they lived at Town Lodge on Saunton Road she would take Uncle Leonard his dinner every day by jumping over several back garden hedges until she arrived at the farmhouse.

The youngest son Sidney was also a big, strong young man who worked at Town Farm and rented land for himself on the Great Field. When the owner of Cross Farm, Robert Perryman, retired in 1937 he offered the tenancy of the farm to Sidney. Cross Farm was another village farm situated on the Chapel Street end of the cross roads close to Sidney's family farm.

Sidney with his wife Evelyn and daughters Nancy and Violet moved into Cross Farm where John Hartnoll

John Hartnoll aged eleven at North Buckland on his Uncle Tom's tractor in 1950.

was born. Tragedy struck two years later in 1941 when Sidney died of pneumonia at the age of thirty-nine.

The tenancy died with Sidney and so Evelyn moved to Station Road with her young family. But it was wartime and low flying aircraft plus the threat of being bombed made them move back to Evelyn's family home at Broadgate Farm at North Buckland. Evelyn's brother Tom and his wife Nancy had two farms at North Buckland, Broadgate and Forest Farm, and when I met Nancy at her home at Forest House she told me how she remembers Violet came to help her every day on the farm. And as can be seen by the photograph, young John loved to help his Uncle Tom with the tractor work.

John was very much involved with the Young Farmers' Clubs and would attend as many events and occasions as possible. It was at these events that John met Jane Leworthy who lived with her parents on their farm near Barbrook on Exmoor.

At the Annual Rally John had watched Jane take part in the competitions held during the day. In the evening at the dance held at Bromley's Ballroom in Barnstaple, Jane was awarded first prize in the dress-making and modelling competition for which she was most pleased. John said he was more interested in her skills as a sheep shearer! Both talents came into their own in the years to come.

John and Jane married in 1965 at Lynton and moved into Forrest House, North Buckland with John's mother Evelyn.

In 1966 Evelyn died and John's Uncle Ernest was ill with arthritis and so offered John to take over Town Farm.

They later moved to Town Lodge where they brought up their four children, David, Gill, Dawn and Rebecca.

Jill is a chartered accountant who lives in Manchester, Dawn is a teacher in San Fransisco and

Rebecca is a freelance theatrical costume maker specializing in leather and metal work.

The family moved to Broadlands Farm on the edge of the Great Field in 1986. John both owns and rents land on Braunton Marshes and the Great Field and sits on the Board of Inspectors for both of these ancient and historic areas of Braunton. John told me that in the early twentieth century there were approximately 140 farmers who owned and rented land on the Great Field and today there are no more than five!

David now runs Broadlands Farm with his father John and along with the traditional farming is branching out with a selection of vegetables and asparagus which love the rich sandy soil of the area.

Until a few years ago Jane was a partner in the business and worked alongside John growing and harvesting crops as well as tending to the cattle and sheep, and of course sheep-shearing with which she made such an impression on John fifty years ago!

Jane also reflected on those days during the early potato harvest and haymaking in June and then later

John, Jane and David Hartnoll with Jimmy Summerfield and Ernest Hartnoll taking a break at Town Farm.

Mrs Gammon and David Hartnoll watching the combine harvester at work on the Great Field 1972.

John and David scuffling (weeding) between the rows of mangels in the Great Field.

David watches his father John at work lifting potatoes at Broadlands Farm.

the corn harvest when she would prepare and take pasties, cakes and sandwiches out to the workers in the fields.

The long nights of lambing came back to Jane when she took her turn in the two hourly inspections of the sheep in the sheds. In between these visits she sat at the kitchen table and made her daughters dresses or ran up a pair of curtains. So those days of the Young Farmers Club have never gone amiss!

John and Jane Hartnoll at home at Broadlands Farm.

Cross Farm

After the death of Sidney Hartnoll in 1941 the tenancy was handed on to William Avery who came from Knowle where his family had farmed for generations. I met with his son John who told me the history of his farming forebears.

William's wife, Edith, was born at South Burrow Farm on Braunton Marshes, the only child of the Acklands who had been licensees of the Ebrington Arms at Knowle before WWI.

Richard Ackland made his fortune as a rabbit dealer. He employed two men to catch the rabbits. One was called Sandy Clarke of South Street who was an ex-Navy man. The other was a man who lived at Woolacombe and who walked along the coastline to work and arrived at South Burrow in time to throw gravel at Richard's bedroom window to wake him up!

Edith went to Abertawe School run by the Congregational Church in East Street. She left school at fourteen to work as a nanny for a family in Pixie Lane. John thinks she was paid well because when she married William Avery she had saved up £500.

William Avery's family had a farm in the centre of Knowle village. This was cut through the middle when the new Ilfracombe to Barnstaple road was built in the 1920s.

Leaving school at fourteen, William worked on the farm with his brother Philip. There were also two sisters – Minnie, married to Charles Gear who had a music shop in the Square at Braunton, and Jane married Archibald Fossett who worked at Ridges Grocer's shop in High Street, Barnstaple.

After John's Grandfather Avery died his father William and his brother Philip went into partnership with the farm and when William married Edith they moved into the farmhouse. The partnership didn't work out and in 1938 William and his wife Edith took the tenancy of South Dene Farm (near today's Hidden Valley Holiday Park on the A39). They kept cows, pigs and sheep on the steep-sided farm land and produced clotted cream which they supplied to Clarkes Dairy in Braunton. Bert French would arrive at the farm at 5am to collect the cream. The skimmed milk went to feed the pigs.

John Avery's Memories of Life on a Farm

John was eight years old when his family took over the tenancy of Cross Farm and from the earliest age he was expected to help out on the farm, collecting eggs or fetching the cattle from the fields for milking. From the age of eleven he had to do a milk round. Sometimes on summer evenings after tea he would be sent to the Great Field to scuffle (clear the weeds) from between the rows of sugar beet. This would be done with a horse and hoeing implement. There was no time to play with the other lads after school. 'If you were old enough to work – you did!'

Cross Farm as with most of the other farms in the village, had no fields close to it. When the cows were brought in from grazing twice a day for milking, the village streets were alive with them.

He told me that Bill Palmer who had a farm in Gubbins Lane would let his cows out of the farmyard after milking and they would walk on their own to the field at the back of the Beacon. Later on in the morning someone would cycle up to the field and shut the gate!

By the late 1950s traffic through the village had increased considerably and John realised that they could no longer herd the cattle through the streets twice a day. From then on he kept his milking cows down on the marshes and he would travel down there to milk them.

The Great Field

John Avery has had land on the Great Field nearly all his working life. He is passionate about the field, Braunton Marshes and the Burrows and the maintance of them.

John says it must not be forgotten that the Great Field has been continually cultivated for more than 1000 years and therefore it is essential that the crop rotation system is used. Today he mainly grows cereals and potatoes.

When Robert Perryman died his daughter Jessie became the owner of Cross Farm and when she died having no family the farm was eventually sold after a long and well documented legal battle fought by John's son Justin Avery. Today what was the last working village farm is a housing complex.

South Street Farm

Margaret Dudley, the eldest daughter of Fred and Joyce Mitchell, treasures her memories of her maternal grandparents Easton's farm in South Street. They were a seafaring family and Margaret says she felt that she had one foot in the sea on her father's side while over

William Easton of South Street Farm at work on the Great Field.

the back wall of their garden the other foot skipped about in the farmyard in South Street.

The farmyard led all the way down to the railway line. Today this is the village car park. Once it was full of farm implements and carts and the hens would lay their eggs all over the place – on ledges and behind the ricks.

There was an orchard with 'long nose' apple trees which bore pale green sweet apples that looked as if they had been pulled out of shape. During the war their old sheep dog would sit by a basket of these apples that Granny Easton left on the pavement for the servicemen to help themselves. Margaret also remembers that this dog used to be sent to their fields at Vellator to bring the cows back to the farm for milking.

The farm had fields in different parts of the village and Margaret recalls going to Down Lane where they used to grow sugar beet and to the Great Field where they had strips of land. Her mother used to carry out jugs of cider and tea to the fields at harvest time.

Grandfather Easton was an honest, upright man in bearing and character, but on reflection Margaret says the hardest work was done by her grandmother at Barnstaple Pannier market on Fridays, on a cart to sell her produce, milking the cows, making hogs pudding on the huge scrubbed table and cooking always cooking! She recalled being given 'thunder and lightning' (a slice of bread thickly spread with cream and treacle) at the farm and roast potatoes with sugar on them at her other grandmother's at Rose Cottage.

There are more of Margaret's memories in the chapter on Braunton Seafarers.

Warren Farm

Roland Dibble was born 1928 in Barnstaple. His father Charlie Dibble came from Swimbridge and his mother, Ester Squires originated from Atherington.

From as early as nine years old he can remember catching the bus out to Warren Farm at Saunton at weekends to help out the farmer Mr. Packer. When he left school at the age of fourteen in 1942 Roland moved in with the Packer family and worked on the farm full time and has been there from that day to this.

William Easton of South Street Farm with his pal. Bill retired to farming after being a policeman in Bristol.

The Packer Family of Warren Farm – L-R: Dulcie, George, Billy, Gwen and baby Rene sitting on his mother Maud's lap. Maud was a daughter of William and Eliza Lane of Broadgate Farm East Street.

Roland Dibble feeding his sheep on the steep hillside above the Saunton road.

Roland met his wife Josephine who was from Ilfracombe and they married in Braunton in 1956 and moved into the thatched cottage next to the farm.

The farm is owned by the Christie Estates and in 1957 when George Packer died Roland was successful in applying for the tenancy.

Roland reminisces about the salesman at Trumps Seeds who helped him by letting him have corn and seed potatoes and manure on twelve months credit and never sent the bill in for eighteen months and also gave him all the discounts that had occurred. 'Not like it any more,' says Roland, 'It's not unusual to have to pay for your goods before you have them these days.' He also recalls that a farmer's 'office' used to be on the mantle shelf above the fire place. 'The bills would come in and be put on the left hand side of the shelf and then move to the right hand side when they'd been paid!' 'These days you need a room with computers, printers and filing systems

and such things.' Roland added, sometimes when he has forms to fill in and the question is, "What experience do you have," he answers, "A lifetime's experience and you don't get certificates for that!!"

For many years Roland's only horse power on the farm was just that – horses! He's very proud that in 1952 he was the last farmer in the area to buy a tractor for use in the fields. Many fields are very steep as they rise above Saunton beach and horses had a better grip on the ground than tractors.

Roland and his wife Jo lament the passing of Barnstaple Cattle Market. They remember with pleasure taking their cattle and sheep to the market and while Roland did his business with other farmers Jo would go into the town and do her shopping before meeting up with Roland and having lunch sometimes with friends before travelling home. They agreed that much more business was carried out when they personally went to market rather than packing their animals off in the back of a truck to travel all the way to Cornwall or Wales to be sold.

Fred Welch and Frank Harper ploughing at Buckland Barton.

The Welch Family moved from Goodleigh to farm at Buckland Barton in the 1930s. L-R: Blanch and Fred Welch, their sons Fred and Dick and Frank Harper who was a life-long friend of Mr Welch and moved with them to Braunton. In the front of the group is daughter Amy, their other daughter Olena is probably taking the photograph. Olena married Peter Welch of the Braunton seafaring family – confusing!

Chapter 4
The Bulb Farm

A unique feature of Braunton was a farm with no farmhouse and no animals – the Braunton Bulb Farm. Daffodil, tulip and iris culture is usually the domain of the east coast where the soil is better suited to their growth. However, in 1923 the company of Seymour Cobley rented their first field at Sandy Lane which they described as, 'rather poor, rabbit infested sandy soil'.

The Cobley family of North London had farmed for 200 years before diversifying into horticulture. They specialized in daffodil, tulip and iris bulbs and also grew early daffodils for the wholesale market.

Seymour Cobley had farms in Lincolnshire, Hampshire and Scotland and in 1922 Barnstaple Rural District Council received a letter from them asking if there was any land available which would be suitable for a new horticultural venture. That enquiry led to the company renting a 4 acre field in Sandy Lane (at £8 per annum) and was the start of a productive business that lasted nearly fifty years.

The question of why this company would want to start up a business in this part of the world, on land that would need thousands of tons of seaweed, manure and other fertilizers to make it viable for growing flowers, begs to be answered.

Maybe it had something to do with Seymour Cobley being a keen golfer and with England's first golf club, the Royal North Devon, being on the doorstep at Westward Ho! When he moved his family from Hampshire to Northam he was able to indulge his love of golf and have control of his business within a few miles of each other.

In the first year one and a quarter million irises were planted by gangs of workers, with women doing most of the planting. If the crop was to be bulbs, the flower heads were picked off as soon as they formed so the goodness of the plant went back into the bulb. The flower heads were emptied onto the compost heap and what a colourful sight that must have made.

Daffodils were the first crop of the year to be picked as flowers and extra labour swelled the local workforce. The flowers were carefully bunched and packed in boxes and sent by lorry or train to Covent Garden and other large flower markets in the U.K. At peak bloom time 300 workers were needed.

Mrs Evelyn Snell joined Seymour Cobley, and with a background as a horticultural academic became manager of Sandy Lane Farm and later a shareholder and director.

She also purchased and farmed many other acres of land. She successfully reclaimed many acres of sandy soil and built sheds and offices and glass-houses.

During WWII production turned over to, 'feeding the nation' and so the crops were almost all fruit and vegetables. With the men away in the forces the work was taken on by local women and Land Army girls.

Memories of Mrs Snell are varied but most say she was a hard task master. She lived at Willoways and later at Overshortacombe, which had been her mother's home. Both overlooked the bulb fields and with her binoculars she could watch the workers in

Packing bulbs at the Sandy Lane Bulb Farm. Knights Photographers

The lorry being loaded ready to be transported. 'Britain delivers the goods' is written on the side of the boxes. Third from the right is Vera 'Micky' Coates. Knights Photographers

the fields. There are stories of people being given their 'cards' because Mrs Snell could see them having a quiet 'ciggie' behind the sheds, or some other misdeed!

Harry Lovering was the foreman at the Bulb Farm, and his wife Elizabeth was persuaded by Mrs Snell to leave their home and move in with her at Willoways. Elizabeth became the cook and their daughter Evelyn was Mrs Snell's companion.

Some of the hard-working bulb farm girls outside of the many greenhouses.

Evelyn's daughter Christine says her mother told her that when Mrs. Snell had been ill she convalesced at the hospital in Bideford and Evelyn thought it a mammoth journey when she had to travel weekly to Bideford with Mrs Snell's clean clothes, messages and letters.

At the end of WWII Seymour Cobley's nephew Roger joined the staff in the Bideford office. Sometime later, with Mrs Snell still unwell, Roger was allowed to visit the Sandy Lane Farm but he had to telephone ahead of his arrival!

After long bouts of illness Mrs Snell informed the Board that her doctor had told her she must not come back to work for six months so they had better find a man to take her place until she could return. But it was not to be. For soon after, she died. The year was 1953.

George Legge, born in Barnstaple, worked at Brannam's Pottery first as a ball maker (forming balls of clay ready for the potter) and later operating a machine that produced 4000 pots a day. But the monotony of it led the eighteen-year-old to apply for a job at the Bulb Farm.

It was 1954 and George loved being in the open air. He worked with a gang of men digging potatoes, planting and sorting bulbs or picking flowers. In the greenhouses the soil and bulbs had to be sterilized with steam so that no disease could be passed on through the crop. George says he enjoyed all aspects of the work except hedging and ditching.

Planting the bulbs in the fields was back-breaking work, as was picking the flowers when they were in bloom. Horses were used to plough the furrows for the bulbs as they did not compact the ground the way tractors did. Sandy

The men take a well-earned break.

Lane Farm had seven or eight horses at one time.

George explained that you couldn't plant flowers every year in the same field so they would alternate the crops with potatoes, sugar beet, corn, tomatoes and asparagus.

He was often sent to work at other farms or fields at Nethercott, Halsinger and Boode, which were owned or rented by the company. On one occasion he was at Nethercott Farm and the foreman told him to take one of the farm horses, Turpin, back to Sandy Lane Farm. A sack was thrown over the horse's back and George was helped up onto it for what I gather was his first equine experience! George still marvels at the way the horse made his own way back to the farm, stopping at the main Saunton road and looking both ways before crossing. George also remembers every jolt as he sat astride for 3 painful miles!

Another occasion etched on his memory is when he was helping several men to paint the greenhouses and they heard a noise "which sounded like a plane". You can imagine their horror to see a huge swarm of hornets heading towards them. They did as they were told and froze to the spot as the insects flew overhead. The only injured party was a horse which was stung and made off in a panic.

After Mrs Snell's death the directors of Seymour Cobley decided to scale back their Braunton business and over the next two decades dispensed with their leased and rented lands and only kept their Sandy Lane Farm.

In 1963 two events left their mark on the Company. The first was the death of Seymour Cobley. The second – and probably the greater – was the closure of the Braunton Railway line. Flowers now had to be taken to Barnstaple goods station and increasing traffic in the town meant boxes of flowers missed their train and therefore were not in peak condition to get the best prices when they arrived at the markets.

In October 1969 with insurmountable financial losses Roger Cobley had to give notice to his remaining staff and sell the Sandy Lane Bulb Farm. Thus closed a notable chapter in Braunton's history.

Chapter 5
Life Around the Estuary

Braunton Burrows are almost 1500 acres of undulating grass covered sand dunes which extend for 6 miles of golden beach around the Braunton Marshes. They are owned and managed by Christie Devon Estates with some of the land leased to the Ministry of Defence for training. During WWII the Americans used the area to train for the D Day Landings in Normandy. Today the Royal Marines stationed at Chivenor also use it for training.

Due to the rare flora and fauna that can be found in the area it has been designated the country's first Biosphere Reserve. Part of the scheme is to reintro-duce cattle and sheep to graze on the land as a way to manage the growth of scrub. In order to do this, parts of the Burrows have been fenced but gates and stiles have been installed so that the public have access to all areas. Local people as well as visitors appreciate the advantage of such a large, interesting and natural environment.

It is thought that at one time there was a small hamlet in the dunes along with a chapel known as St Anne's but all signs of these have been swept away with the continually shifting sands. The same fate has almost obliterated the lighthouse that stood over-

The lighthouse at Crow Point with its wooden octagonal tower. It housed two families who grew their own fruit and vegetables, kept chickens and had the groceries and water delivered by the ferry from Appledore. R.L. Knight

The last lighthouse keeper at Crow, Redvers Buckler and his wife Iverna and daughter Rita.

looking Crow Beach. The octagonal wooden tower with accommodation for two lighthouse keepers' families below was built in the early 1800s with the hope of saving ships attempting to enter the estuary over the notoriously dangerous sand bar from the Bay.

This main light was known as High Light and there was another light further north which was known as Low Light. When seafarers lined these lights up they knew they were on the correct course to cross the Bar.

Redvers Buckler was one of the lighthouse keepers

A sand barge travels home loaded.

Standing on far right is Henry Mitchell with other bargees on one of the sandbanks in the Taw Estuary.

at Crow and it was here that his wife Iverna gave birth to their daughter Rita who told me of her early years in this beach-front paradise.

She can vividly recall the boats coming over the Bar and watching Tommy Clarke who came down to the beach each day to see how much weight in sand or gravel the barges were carrying and charge the barge-men accordingly.

Before joining Trinity House Redvers had been a carpenter back in his home village of Hartland and he now spent hours making toys for Rita including a dolls house. He was a keen gardener and with a plentiful supply of seaweed for manure he grew vegetables and tomatoes and flowers in their garden beside the lighthouse.

Apart from rainwater their fresh water was brought over from Appledore by Mr Cann in his boat. In those days it was usual to go across to Appledore on a ferry for provisions as it was to walk to Braunton village. A visitor in July 1943 was the Vicar of Apple-dore.

He travelled across with some fishermen and whilst they were trying to catch salmon which, were in very short supply that year he had visited the Buckler family and their dog Micky at the lighthouse, shared in a few prayers and then 'enjoyed a lovely cup of tea and homemade cakes and bread, butter and jam.' The vicar also visited the lantern tower and commented on 'how clean and smart the brass fittings were kept. Well up to the standard that the Trinity Brethren expect of their staff.'

The view over the sandhills reminded him of how the light had guided him safe home when returning from Lundy Island and how they had to keep the two lights in line to avoid hitting the northern shore of the estuary.

After four hours fishing and with each boat having caught only a small salmon they collected the church-man and carried him back across the water to Appledore where he was hoisted on the back of one of the fishermen and delivered back to dry land.

Rita can recall that when she first went to school at Caen Street her father would take her on a Monday morning and to get to the car they had a long walk over the dunes. As this journey took so long at the young age of five she had to board all week with a family in the village.

Sometimes her friend Jean would be invited to spend the weekend with her at the lighthouse and she recalls the time they wandered off into the dunes to play and an American soldier came across them, scooped them up in his arms and took them back to the safety of the lighthouse. This was wartime and the girls soon found that the Yankees were a good source of chewing gum and sweets! Rita can also recall that one time when she was unwell a soldier brought her some tinned fruit which English children had never known.

In 1945 the lighthouse was deemed too unsafe for the families to live there anymore and Rita and her parents moved back to Hartland. The light became redundant in 1957 when a new unmanned light was erected at the southern tip of Crow Point.

This area of Crow Point and the beaches are very popular especially with local people. There is an expanse of unspoilt beach and sand dunes to let dogs and children run free, kick balls, hunt for sea urchins in the pools, fly kites, swim in the shallow waves, picnic, read a book or fish for bass in the pools before the incoming tide gives you wet feet and trousers!

The estuary and Crow beach were once very plentiful for catching fish and especially salmon when it was in season. One such fisherman was Sidney Crick, born at Vellator in 1912. By the age of six along with his brother Jan they were accompanying their father Henry Abbot Crick collecting shell fish on the River Taw and in the summer months they would

Left: *Sid Crick, salmon fisherman with one of his catch.*
Right: *After WWII Sid became an officer with H.M. Customs at Plymouth.*

fish for salmon as his father had a licence. (Only a limited number were issued each year which led to some illicit sales of salmon!) The family also collected large amounts of seaweed which was taken to the Bulb Farm in Sandy Lane to be used as manure.

Like many others, at the age of fourteen Sidney went to sea on a Welsh boat that came into Vellator delivering coal. At eighteen he joined the Merchant Navy and gained his certificate as a bosun. Commissioned into the Royal Navy during WWII he captained a mine sweeper working in the North Sea. After the war he became a Customs Officer in Plymouth.

He later returned to his roots and came back to Vellator and skippered a sand barge collecting sand for a local builder. When his father died he took over his salmon licence and carried on fishing late into his life. He died at the age of ninety-two in 2004. A well-known Braunton character who could be correctly said was 'Salt of the Earth'.

Sid Crick mending his salmon nets.

A study of a contented man – Sid takes home his day's catch.

Another Mitchell family of South Street whose working life was centred around the sand barges and salmon fishing. Taken in 1904/5 at their home at North View, 19, South Street: L-R back row: Frank Mitchell b.1893, Annie b.1885, Susie b.1883, Henry b.1891 (Maurice Clements' grandfather). Seated: Father John Mitchell b. 1862, mother Elizabeth b.1866, baby John (Jack) b.1904, Isabella b.1888. On the ground: Hilda b.1899 and Lizzie Jane b.1896 died 14.6.10.

Above: *Tommy Clarke, Henry Mitchell and Jack Mitchell pull in their nets.*

Left: *Henry Mitchell with his catch in the Taw Estuary.*

Hauling in their salmon nets.

A good day's work!

Henry Mitchell and his dog Prince coming home up the Pill on his sandbarge Hilda.

Smudger Smith often went fishing with John Thorpe in his trawler **Freedom**. *They would later sell their catch from a box on John's doorstep at his cottage at Vellator.*

This photo shows two battling campaigners who fought long and hard with every authority that came their way. Tommy Slee and Henry Mitchell declared that the gates along Sandy Lane and through the burrows leading to Crow Point should not be locked. However, the owners of the land insisted that the gates be locked. Tommy and Henry would regularly drive along the lane and cut the locks off the gates. This silent protest went on for a long time with people of substance taking up the cause on both sides until eventually a court ruling in 1976 confirmed that this was a right of way with free access for all.

Back in the mists of time this was a direct route from Saunton to the ferry to Appledore. Also farmers used the lane to gather seaweed to use as fertilizer on the Great Field. And the route had to be left open to transport coal to the lighthouse. Nowadays of course none of these reasons apply but the two old gentlemen won their day!

Chapter 6

The Seafaring Community

With the sea coming up to the doorstep of Braunton it is understandable that seafaring became the life blood of many local families. And although Vellator is no longer a working port there are still many leisure boats in and around the Pill.

On a quiet sunny day the ghosts of the sailing ketches, schooners and barques of 150 years ago can be imagined once again loading and unloading their cargoes which have been plied along the coast of England, Wales and Ireland.

What is amazing is how popular the ports of Braunton, Barnstaple, Bideford and Appledore were in their heyday in the hundred years from 1850 despite the dangers of entering the Taw-Torridge Estuary over Bideford Bar.

The Bar is where the sea narrows between the opposite shores of Northam and Braunton Burrows and is a bank of sand and gravel which extends for more than a mile. At low tide the water level can be only 3ft. But when the wind is blowing strongly from the west and with a heavy groundswell the sea becomes a raging torrent with a rumbling roar that all of us living within the Taw and Torridge area are well aware of.

During the eighteenth and nineteenth centuries the number of sailing ships coming to grief whilst negotiating the Bar was horrendous. Even after a lighthouse was built at Crow Point and another navigational light was installed in 1822 the ship-wrecks did not diminish by many. At night the mariners had to line up the two lights before trying to navigate over the Bar. Often the crew roped them-selves to the mast or rigging to avoid being washed overboard whilst negotiating the rough water.

Vellator Quay in 2014.

Ships at Vellator when it was a busy working port.

The Enid *tied up at Vellator with Braunton in the distance.*

The ketch the Enid.

Lifeboats played a significant part in rescues. The Appledore lifeboat, *Volunteer* was the first boat in action and later in 1833 a 26 foot lifeboat called *Assistance* was stationed at the Braunton side of the estuary. In 1857 the *Dolphin* was the first RNLI lifeboat stationed at Braunton but the station was known as Appledore No.3. No doubt this was because the crew all came from Appledore although the horses that pulled the lifeboat into the water were owned and ridden by Braunton farmers.

The lifeboat crew had to row across from Appledore to Crow Point and then race along the beach to the lifeboat station. At the same time a signal was sent from the lighthouse to Braunton village so the farmers could harness their horses (up to ten of them) and ride them out to the beach to tow the lifeboat into the sea. It is no wonder that during the time it took to carry out the launch a ship came to grief and broke up with many lives lost. Not occasionally but continually, sometimes several times in one day!

The last Braunton lifeboat was the *Robert and Catherine* which took up station in 1912. She was best known for her rescue of four crew mem-

bers from a schooner bound from Cork which rolled over and broke up.

In 1914 with many farmers and horses being sent to France to fight in WWI the Braunton lifeboat had to be suspended. Then the decision was made to close it permanently.

In the early years of the twentieth century with better navigational aids and the installation of engines the number of ships coming to grief over the Bar slowly diminished although it is still a dangerous place to negotiate.

Before the new quay was built in the 1850s most of the sea going vessels that used Vellator were small coastal boats that plied their trade in and around the South West peninsula. Now many local seafaring

Above: *Crow lighthouse with ships going over the Bar.*

Wreck of the Phyllis Gray *on Saunton Sands 9 September, 1908.*

Braunton lifeboat Jane Hannah MacDonald *at Saunton in 1904 with the Appledore crew and the Braunton and Saunton horses and men.*

A ghostly view of the past, at Braunton Pill.

families purchased larger vessels and set out to trade further afield. They travelled along the coast of France, Belgium, Holland and Germany. Names such as *Bessie Clark*, the *Result*, and *Bessie Ellen* transported agricultural produce from Vellator and returned with coal, timber, flour, cattle cake and salt.

The Mitchell Family

Bill Mitchell is from a family steeped in sea going history. I visited him at the home of his birth at Station Road and he shared with me many of his memories. He told me that from the time he was little more than a toddler his father, who had been the skipper of the ketch *Agnes* since 1924, would take him for long days out. Just the two of them and he reckons this was to prepare him for being away from the home and family when and if he wanted to go to sea.

Life at sea for Bill began when he was six years old and went on his first voyage to the port of Lydney which is as far as these ships could travel up the River Severn. They loaded up with coal, returning to the North Devon coast and delivering it to Watermouth Cove. Coal, basic slag or flour was also carried from Swansea to Barnstaple and Bideford.

Discharging coal at Watermouth Cove was no easy task as they had to catch a spring tide – a high tide. The higher the tide the further up the beach the sea travels and therefore the higher the boat can be beached. With the *Agnes* high and dry the coal merchant from Combe Martin could bring his lorries alongside the vessel. Two of the crew in the hold loaded large wicker baskets and then these were winched onto the deck where another crew member would empty the coal down a chute into the waiting lorry. With 100 tons of coal to move between the two tides, which is approximately eight hours, it is easy to understand how hard these men had to work.

William Mitchell, his father Samuel John Mitchell and grandfather Frank Mitchell.

Two of William's brothers George and Frank Mitchell.

Mary Jane Mitchell – Samuel's wife and mother to William, George, Frank John and Fred.

Fred Mitchell.

William Mitchell and his wife Nora and children Vera and Bill in the back garden of the Mitchell family home, Rose Cottage in South Street.

The bow of the Agnes.

The 45 ton ketch Agnes, built in 1904 at Bude. The master – William Mitchell. Photo taken in 1938.

The wash away from the bow of the Agnes.

Bill told me about the last time they were able to unload on the beach at Watermouth Cove. It was in September 1942 and there was a build-up of military personnel on the road above them. Later an Army Sergeant approached the boat and barked at them that they were lucky they hadn't been shot out of the water the night before when they entered the cove as it was out of bounds at night.

Before WWII Bill recalls that at spring tides they would carry as much as 300 tons of flour up the River Yeo at Barnstaple where lorries would be waiting to take it to bakeries. On the return journey they would load up with English wheat at Stanbury's Mill for transport to Wales and then back again with a load of cattle cake. And so it would go on.

In 1942 Bill went to sea full time at the age of thirteen. Sailing through the Bristol Channel in the war years was terrifying for grown men let alone young boys. The Channel was a mine-field and a minesweeper was always on patrol to blow up the mines.

By the age of fifteen Bill's father told him that with all the older men away at the war he'd have to become the ship's mate. Soon after this Captain Mitchell took on another fifteen year old, Harry Ridge, as the cook. This meant the Agnes was traveling with a crew of three lads under the age of sixteen and Bill was showing them how to sail and the ways of the sea! However this would have been second nature to Bill as a year earlier when his father had been taken ill at sea, Bill had to take over as the master of the *Agnes* with only one crew member.

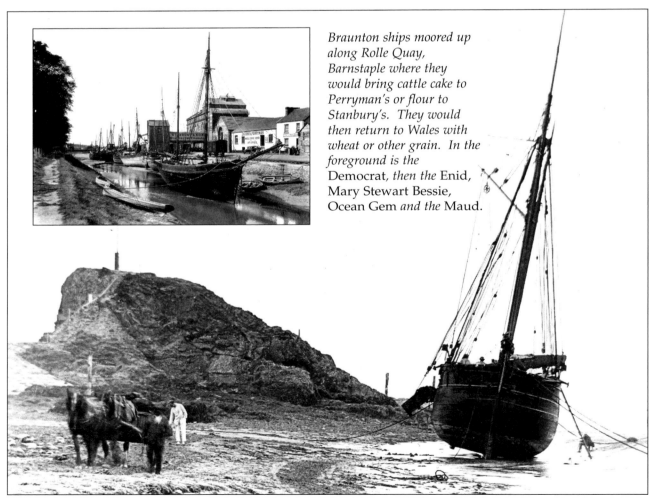

Braunton ships moored up along Rolle Quay, Barnstaple where they would bring cattle cake to Perryman's or flour to Stanbury's. They would then return to Wales with wheat or other grain. In the foreground is the Democrat, *then the* Enid, Mary Stewart Bessie, Ocean Gem *and the* Maud.

This is how the ship discharged coal on the beach at Watermouth. (This vessel is the Ceres *at Bude.)*

Agnes loaded with wheatfeed (bran) for Avonmouth at Barry Dock in 1955.

Cleaning out the hold of the Agnes.

Once when traveling through the Bristol Channel, Bill saw a sight he will never forget – hundreds of ships anchored, loaded to their gunnels and every one of them had a barrage balloon attached to it. As the *Agnes* wended its way between them, without any noise or warning suddenly all the ships upped anchor and slid slowly past them. Later they learnt that these ships were being taken across the English Channel to play their part in the D Day Landings.

In 1952 Bill Mitchell senior retired and Bill took over the *Agnes* as skipper but by now the work for ketches like the *Agnes* were becoming few and far between due to the improved road system and larger lorries that were much cheaper to run and could move the cargoes by road from door to door.

Sadly more and more vessels were being laid up or sold and so inevitably the time came when the owners of the *Agnes* (Bill's father being one of them) decided to sell her. Three years later in 1958 she was wrecked near Barbados.

Bill regrets the demise of the coastal traders as it was the only life he knew and he loved every minute of it. Mostly he had enjoyed the early days when he was taking cargoes to river ports or beaches like Watermouth Cove or Caldy Island. In fact one of his last trips was to deliver coal to the monks on Caldy Island, just off the Pembrokshire coast. He said that he remembers so clearly that he had to beach the *Agnes* as the tide ebbed. Several monks came on board and threw the coal over the side onto the beach and then loaded it onto a tractor and trailer. They hadn't finished when the tide came in so Bill had to weigh anchor just off the island until the next day when the *Agnes* went back to the beach and the monks came back on board and removed the last of the coal and cleaned out the hold by washing it out with water hauled up from over the side. After discharging every cargo the hold had to be scrubbed clean as a cargo of flour quite often followed a cargo

of basic slag or manure!

After my research of wrecks on the Bideford/Barnstaple Bar I naturally asked Bill Mitchell what it was like negotiating the Bar when it was at its most aggressive. He told me: "The worst occasion I can remember when crossing the Bar was in 1947 when we came out of Rolle Quay in Barnstaple loaded with wheat for Swansea. Bill Stribling, a Barnstaple pilot, came with us to negotiate the sandbanks in the River Taw and I rowed him ashore to Instow as was usual".

"Once back on board we set sail in a light southerly wind for the open sea but too late to turn back when we could see the violent ground swell causing huge

Ship broker's bill.

breakers over the Bar. All we could do was ride our way through the ferocious water like riding a bucking bronco, knowing only too well that one wrong move and we were done for".

After the *Agnes* was sold Bill went to work with his Uncle Fred Mitchell on his sand barge *JJRP*. No more crossing the Bar or traveling up and down the coast now Bill and his uncle took the *JJRP* out into the Taw Estuary at full tide and ground it on a sand bank. Then the two men would shovel sand and gravel into the barge until the tide came back in to lift it off the bottom. Then off home again to shovel it all out of the barge onto Vellator Quayside. Sometimes they could dig as much as 60 tons a day on Crow Point. And it has been known for the two of them to fill the barge in just two hours!

Beatrice with son Samuel John.

Bill's family came from a long line of seafarers. His father William had four brothers, George, Frank, John and Fred, all of whom made their living from the sea as did their father Samuel and their grandfather Frank. Bill's great-grandfather went to sea as a young lad on windjammers and travelled the globe. In fact he didn't come back home for eight years and when he did his own mother didn't recognise him and sent this 'stranger' packing when he came into the house!

To continue with the Mitchell family story, I visited Dorothy Davies whose father was George Mitchell. George was a Mate on the *Maud*, *Result* and *Traly*. When one of his boats called in at Chivenor Farm he met his future wife Beatrice Page, where her father was a gamekeeper and forester.

Beatrice had Dorothy and a son Samuel but sadly she died aged thirty-three years in 1933 when there was an epidemic of TB in Braunton. Dot was only eight years old and Sam was five.

Dot and Sam went to Caen Street School where she remembers very strict school life until she left at the age of thirteen. Dot remembers that Sam loved gardening and as the school grew its own vegetables the boys would be called out of lessons to help in the gardens. Dot says this absence from schooling was not a disappointment for Sam!

In a filmed interview with Sam and his fellow shipmate Len Baglole they tell of the hard times they endured during their life at sea. However, it is obvious that they had many happy memories and had preserved an excellent sense of humour.

They both tell stories of having to cope with always being wet and the decks always awash. Sam said he'd have all his oil skins on and climb up the ladder

from below, pull back the hatch and that was the very moment a wave would break over the deck and he'd be swamped. He'd then have to work with just as much sea water on the inside of his clothes as on the outside!

Food on board was another subject that caused hilarity. Sam said the skipper was responsible for purchasing the victuals and the less he spent on the food the more he kept in his pocket. There was salt bacon and salted beef which they would tie on a piece of rope and hang over the side of the boat to get the salt out of it. Then there was Toe Rag – dried and salted cod which they would soak and boil to get as much salt out of it as possible before frying it. Sam informs us that all these dried foods would

Dorothy and Sam Mitchell after their mother had died of T.B. aged thirty-three. Sam went to live with his grandparents in South Street and Dorothy went to live with an aunt in Cornwall. She returned to Braunton when her father married again.

Sid Crick, Sam Mitchell and Len Baglole taking a walk down memory lane when they visited the Kathleen and May *when she was being refitted at Bideford.*

Margaret and Jillian Mitchell give their father Fred a hand to fill his sand barge!

be hung from the ceiling of the galley for months with everyone smoking under it! They both agreed that they were always hungry and so ate whatever was given them – and enjoyed it.

When asked if they'd ever fallen overboard, they both replied 'Never' and Len added 'Because it's a long walk home if you did'!

Climbing the rigging was obviously not an enviable task either. One hand held on to the rigging and the other did the work, but sometimes you needed two hands to work and then you had to hold on with your teeth!

Both of these sea dogs recalled the happy times when they'd witness half a dozen or more ships going up the estuary to Barnstaple on one tide. And Len added that if the same thing happened again you

wouldn't be able to get on Rolle Quay for the thousands of people that would be there to see these grand old ships again.

Fred Mitchell was the youngest of Sam Mitchell's five sons. During WWII he joined the Merchant Navy and took part in salvaging planes and boats sunk in and around the coastline. After the war he joined the deep sea oil tankers and travelled worldwide. He returned home and bought the gravel barge *JJRP* and worked with both his nephews Bill and Sam at different times in the age old trade of collecting sand and gravel from the Taw Estuary.

Fred married Joyce Eastern and they had three daughters Margaret, Jillian and Kathleen. Margaret recalls her Grandfather Sam Mitchell lived for making model boats which filled his cottage. The doors in the cottage were painted with boats, roses and sometimes a compass. Shell pictures filled the walls and silver pistols hung over the Bodley fire grate. She also writes of her times spent with her father on the river:

'It must have rained then, but my memories are of hot sunny days. I can still smell the hot tar between the boards on the front of the deck as we children sprawled out in the sun and watched the deep colours of the water as we chugged along.

'Food was very important to us and the bargemen. The bargemen looked forward to their breakfast of fried fat bacon and cold potatoes as they waited for the tide to go out and the barge to rest on the gravel sand banks.'

'The work of loading the barge was steady and to a rhythm – with their backs to the barge the men used long shovels digging into the wet sand then throwing it over their shoulders into the hold. Once the barge was full the hatches were battened down and pegged with tarpaulin and we waited for the tide to float us off the sand bank. The small sounds of the lapping

Fred Mitchell and his barge the JJRP *– waiting to settle on the sandbank as the tide goes out.*

Fred Mitchell in his shed at his home at Tralee, Barton Lane.

water are still a lovely memory as gradually the barge rocked and then floated'.

'As well as collecting gravel Father would pick cockles and gather Laver seaweed which Mother would wash many times before cooking. And of course there was also the fish – salmon, flat fish and all sorts. There was always a gun on board the boat so on occasions we'd have wild duck for dinner!'

'On days when the tides were wrong Father would help out on the farm owned by my mother's family in South Street. Strength was the main thing that barge-men had to have and I remember strong arm competitions being held in the farm barn. This included bending nails, picking up weights in a blanket with their teeth and of course weight lifting. My sister Kathleen who was then a hefty five year old was hoisted up in a blanket by a man's little finger.'

Born on 6 March 1907 Frederick Lane Mitchell died in 2000 leaving a deep impression of the love of the sea in his daughters.

The Seafaring Welch and Clarke Family

Welch is another well-known seafaring name in Braunton with many associations with other seago-ing and ship-owning families.

Today Tom Welch and his wife Joyce have a farm in the neighbouring Ashford parish. Tom has both the sea and the soil in his gene pool. His father's family

have been related to the sea for centuries but his maternal family were farmers. Their story can be found in the Farming chapter.

Although Tom's life is now firmly on the soil his interest and knowledge of sea-going vessels is vast, especially those that traded out of Vellator such as the schooner *Result* which both his father Peter and grandfather Thomas owned and mastered at different times.

Although Tom can trace his family back several generations we will start with his great-great-grand-parents Captain Thomas and Mrs Anne Clarke who lived at Wrafton. They had at least nine children: three of the sons were Thomas, who was lost at sea at the age of seventeen, George and John, and three daughters Jane, Emily and Elizabeth.

Elizabeth married James Welch, a wheelwright on the Fortescue Estate at Simonsbath. They had three sons George, William and Thomas Clarke Welch.

When he was twelve Thomas was caught poaching salmon from a river on the estate and it was decided that he should be sent to live at Braunton with his mother's sister Jane and her husband Henry S.G. Clarke at Hillside, East Hill.

Aunt Jane and Uncle Harry Clarke did not have any children and soon found that Thomas was an inconvenience to them and so his schooling came to an abrupt end and he was sent to sea on the *Bessie Clarke*, a vessel they owned on which Robert Tucker was master.

Thomas remained with Captain Bob on the *Bessie Clarke* for four years and then was taken on as crew with the deep-sea, square-rigged ship *Castleton*, bound for the west coast of South America which involved rounding Cape Horn, with a cargo of coal.

It was 1909 and Henry Clarke was having the *Democrat* built. He also purchased the three masted schooner *Result* for £1000. Thomas joined the ship as Mate.

He stayed with the *Result* for a few months until the *Democrat* was finished and he then joined her as her Master.

Within the year the *Democrat* was involved in a very sad incident on the 13 October, 1910, when unloading coal just off the Pembrokshire coast.

The Result.

Capt. Thomas Clarke and his wife Ann Clarke née Gent of Wrafton. Photo taken in 1870.

James and Elizabeth Welch née Clarke.

The Welch family at Simonsbath. L-R: Sons, William and Thomas, mother Elizabeth, father James and other son George.

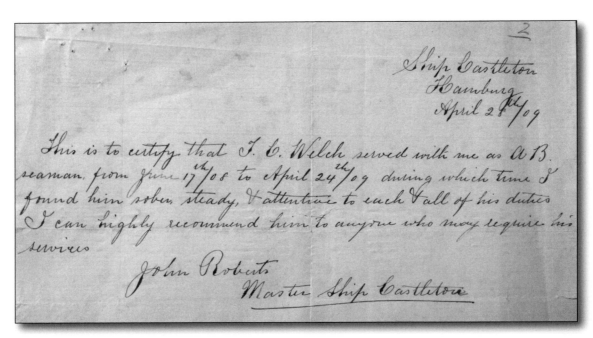

A reference letter for Thomas C. Welch.

The Result *after she had had her main mast removed in 1954.*

The Democrat.

There was no quay to off load the coal on to so the operation was being carried out with the use of a breeches buoy. The local lifeboat *Gem* – a 12 oared sailing boat from St David's – came out to them and advised them to leave because of the weather conditions. The crew of the *Democrat* said they were OK and continued with their work. When the lifeboat came out again they anchored the *Democrat* and the crew of Thomas Welch the Master, Sam Mitchell the Mate and Dendle went aboard the lifeboat.

On the way back to the mainland the lifeboat was swept across the rocks and broke up and sank. The crews of the *Democrat* and the *Gem* clung to the rocks all night.

A lifeboat from Fishguard tried but could not get near the stranded sailors because of the raging sea conditions. Then two local fishermen, Sydney Mortimer and Elenzar James in an 18 ft. boat rowed out to the rocks and picked up the survivors. Sadly Coxwain Stevens and crew members Henry Rowlands and James Price lost their lives. Ironically the *Democrat* sat calmly where she had been left the night before.

The two fishermen went to Buckingham Palace and received the Silver Gallantry Medal.

The *Democrat* continued under the same ownership plying her trade until 1954 when tragedy struck. To be told later in this chapter.

During his life time Henry S. G. Clarke founded the Braunton Electric Light and Power Company. He also headed up a ship owners' insurance company in 1898 which served Braunton and Appledore for many years.

Leaving Henry S. G. Clarke and returning to the life of his nephew Thomas Clarke Welch. It was while he was the Master of the *Democrat* that Thomas went to West Wales, to collect stone and became friendly with ship owner and farmer John Russan.

When Thomas was in the vicinity of John's home he would invite Thomas to stay with the family and on one occasion when the *Democrat* had been laid up for temporary repairs John took Thomas for a stroll and put it to him that if he was of a mind to ask his daugh-

The crew and survivors of the St David's Disaster in 1910 when the lifeboat Gem *wrecked with the loss of the coxswain and two crew members. The 15 survivors spent fourteen hours on the wave-lashed rocks until they were rescued by two fishermen in their rowing boat.*

ter Frances for her hand in marriage now was a good time to do it. As the *Democrat* had to return to Appledore for repairs they could treat those six weeks as the couple's honeymoon! To which Frances, who had been listening from behind the garden hedge, appeared and demanded to know if anyone was going to ask her what her plans for the future held!

We can only presume that Frances was happy to go along with her father's proposal because the couple married on 21 November 1916 and sailed on the *Democrat* back to Appledore. On the first evening out at sea they had had their meal at around 6pm and when her husband started to prepare for bed she asked when supper would be served. Thomas explained that after the evening meal there was no more food served. 'That's not good enough Tom' she said, 'On the farm we always have supper at 9 o'clock and that's what I'm used to so that's the way we'll continue.'

When the couple were at Appledore it was a lonely existence for Frances as her husband would leave home early morning and she wouldn't see him again until the men packed up work at the end of the day. She said she was left alone in a house and village, with people she didn't know. However, love blossomed in Braunton where they lived at No. 4 East

Peter and Olena Welch née Welch of Buckland Barton.

Thomas Welch's family. Standing L-R: *Frances Sylvia, Peter Russan, James Thomas, John and Elizabeth Millicent.* Seated: *Thomas Clarke Welch and his wife Frances Annie Welch née Russan.*

Street and brought up their five children Frances Sylvia, Peter Russan, James Thomas Clarke, John and Elizabeth Millicent.

Their youngest daughter Betty who became a farmer's wife, says her mother was not only a wonderful mother and home-maker but an astute businesswoman. When Sidney Incledon, a principal shareholder and Master of the *Result* died, Frances made haste to the widow's home in South Street and bought his shares much to the other ship's shareholders' chagrin!

It has become obvious to me that although the men were at the helm of these trading vessels their women were definitely at the helm of their businesses!

Peter Welch married Olena Welch, a farmer's daughter from Buckland Barton and they had three children Peter, Tom and Sara. Peter went to work with his father on the *Result* and Tom joined the Merchant Navy until 1977 when he came home to roost and married Joyce a farmer's daughter from Ashford and decided to become a landlubber and put his farming genes to the test.

The *Result* was the last schooner to leave Braunton and is now a museum ship in Ireland.

Another person connected to the *Democrat* and the *Result* was Barbara Price's father Arthur Collings. Barbara told me that her father was a rebel and although his parents had a life planned for him in their grocery shop in the Square in Braunton he had other plans and ran off to sea when he was fifteen years old.

Identity and Service Certificate for Arthur Collings.

He joined the *Democrat* in 1919 and the *Result* in 1921 but when the shipping trade died due to road transport Arthur returned and became a grocer with a shop in Ilfracombe. However, the call of the sea was still too great and he sold the shop and joined the Navy.

Barbara's maternal grandfather was another well-known and respected mariner, Captain Bernard Drake Tucker, who owned the ketch *F.A.M.E.* along with his wife Emma Jane. The boat was named after the four daughters of Richard Hill the builder – Fanny, Anna, Maria and Elizabeth! She was lost off Morte Point in 1929 but all the crew were rescued.

Capt. Bernard Drake Tucker and his wife. He owned the vessel F.A.M.E.

Captain George Coats

George Coats lived with his wife Annie and five children – Gwen, George, Mary, Jack and Vera, at 22, South Street. George, known locally as Captain Coats, worked on the coasters out of Vellator including the ketch *Democrat* which he bought after it stopped trading in 1954.

Brian Norman and his cousin Graham Jenkins told me how they idolised their grandfather Captain Coats and loved to listen to his tales of his life at sea.

Graham obviously loved his grandparents' house with its large back garden and orchard that went all the way down to the railway line and was very sad when it was taken to build today's village car park.

Brian says it was his grandfather that gave him his sea legs as from the age of twelve years he was invited to go along with Captain Coats on his trips on the *Democrat*. Many of their voyages were to transport coal to Porlock Weir and Brian loved these trips because they would dock at Porlock and Brian would be allowed to stay there with his friend Raymond Ley until his grandfather returned with the load of coal.

One other magical moment Brian recalls was when his grandfather set the tiller and let him steer the ship. Mind you he had to stand on a box to do it but he said that experience gave him his thrill of the sea and a foretaste of the career that lay ahead of him.

The *Democrat* was known to have the best food in the Bristol Channel and it was helped by Captain Coats having several relatives who were butchers! Also he was well known and liked at all the trading ports along the Bristol Channel.

When the *Democrat* was unloaded there was always residue in the hold that had to be cleared away before the new cargo was taken on board. On occasions there was an arrangement with some people whereby payment for 'removing' the surplus goods from the hold was rewarded by a sack of food being handed aboard at some later date!

The *Result* in a film

The premier of the film Outcast of the Islands *held at the Gaumont Cinema Barnstaple. L-R: Captain Peter Welch, owner of the* Result*, Sam Mitchell and Darcy Andrews and the manager of the cinema.*

The Result *was renamed 'Flash' for a film called* Outcast of the Islands *which was made in the Isle of Scilly in 1952 and starred Trevor Howard. As Thomas Welch had died in 1948 his son Peter was now the owner and Master of the* Result *and the Mate was Sam Mitchell.*

Right: The ship's crew who were in the film. L-R: Darcy Andrews, Tommy Christie, Sid Crick, Peter Welch (Master), Tommy Slade and Sam Mitchell (Mate).

Another escapade was when Captain Coats and two others drove to Porlock to deliver a large salmon to the chef at the hotel. The price was agreed and the three men were paid over the counter. When they arrived back in Braunton three sheets to the wind – using the nautical term – they found the salmon still in the back of the car!!

The cousins also told me the tale of Captain Coats' 'Friday Pills'. When he had retired he always liked to go to Barnstaple on a Friday as this was market day when everyone from the surrounding countryside would attend the Cattle and Pannier Markets and a good time had by all. The ladies did their week's shopping and the men did their business whether it clerical or buying and selling, after which they all met up for lunch be it a hearty meal or the liquid variety!

During one of these libation lunches in the North Country Inn the Captain was relating his long and varied sea-going career to the surrounding company. Sitting with him were his old sea mates Tommy and Ernie Stribling and Ernie said, 'You've a wonderful memory Capt'n but I make it that you must be 103 years old'!

Brian and Graham said that even if their grandfather had been in bed all week complaining of his ill health, come Friday morning he would be spruced up and raring for the off to Barnstaple Market. And the saying in the family was, 'Its market day the Captain's had his Friday Pills!'

After doing an engineering apprenticeship Brian joined the Merchant Navy as an engineering officer and worked on large ocean-going ships until 1963 when he came home to Braunton.

To complete the tale of Captain Coats I will tell the eerie thing that happened when his grandson

L-R: *Porlock Harbour Master, Arthur Ley, Capt. George Coats and Preston Ley.*

Capt. George Coats with his wife Annie and eldest daughter Gwen.

Gwen Coats outside the family home, 22 South Street.

Jack, Vera (Micky) and George Coats.

The Democrat entering Porlock Weir.

Graham met me at the Braunton Museum to tell me how much his grandfather regretted selling his boat the *Democrat*. He sold it to a couple from Jersey who had asked him several times to sell it to them and eventually he agreed.

Overhearing our conversation Jane Fewings the Museum administrator remembered that a lady had come in the week before with some newspaper cuttings about the sinking of the *Democrat* which had seen three people drowned and left two children orphaned and a woman without her husband and their three children without their father. It was only after she had gone that Jane realised that this lady had been one of the children – Pamela the daughter of William and Joan Sawyer of Gorey, Jersey, the couple who had owned the boat and had drowned along with their engineer Albert Le Toureur

The report in the newspaper article told the story of how Captain Coats only sold the ketch reluctantly to the Sawyers as they wanted to carry on coastal trading between Jersey and the French coast. They had sailed from Appledore but had had to put into port on the Isles of Scilly because of rough weather.

The next time the *Democrat* was seen was by fishermen on the Normandy coast when it was caught in high seas and driven onto a submerged reef called The Antelopes 2 miles from the shore. A tug was sent out to help with the rescue but it was too late: Mr and Mrs Sawyer and Ms Le Toureur were all drowned and the *Democrat* wrecked.

The Chichester Family

Eddie Chichester, the last in his line of Chichesters, told me the story that has been passed down through the family relating to his grandfather John Squire Chichester. John, was working as the Master on the *Mary* of Lynmouth when he had an argument with the owner who asked him to sail on a Sunday which was against John's religious belief. He promptly left his employ and walked all the way home to Braunton.

In the summer of 1906 John Chichester arrived in Plymouth to pick up a cargo and heard about a 150-ton ship that was being built and so he went along to inspect her and bought her.

Raymond Ley and Brian Norman at Porlock Weir where they spent many happy summer days together.

Brian Norman as a Merchant Navy Engineering Officer.

The ship was launched in 1907. His two daughters Ellen, who was thirteen, and Bessie, eleven, went with him to Plymouth where Ellen named the ship *Bessie Ellen* and Bessie broke the bottle of wine over her bow. Their job done, the two girls were promptly packed off back home by train!

The homeward journey for the *Bessie Ellen* was anything but plain sailing as the weather conditions meant the vessel took eleven days to reach Bideford. However, she soon proved to be an excellent sailing boat and a good work-horse.

In May 1920 Captain John Chichester had his wife Bessie and young son Reuben on board with him. They were slowly manoeuvring into Sharpness lock when John noticed that the *Bessie Ellen's* tender which they were towing was in danger of being run down by a large barge following them into the lock. John jumped down into the small boat and moved it. As he was climbing back on board, the barge hit the *Bessie Ellen*, trapping John against the side of his ship. He managed to climb back onto the deck and made his way to his cabin where his wife Bessie called for help. John was taken to hospital but tragically he died the next day.

Bessie Chichester now had to carry on the business and the captaincy of the *Bessie Ellen* passed to their eldest son Jack who had always wanted to have a career at sea although his father had wanted him to have a good education and become an architect. Jack stayed with the *Bessie Ellen* until he went to Littlehampton as master of another sailing ship. He died in 1973.

In 1947 the *Bessie Ellen* was sold to Christian Mollar a Dane who had come to Braunton looking for a sound wooden-hulled boat to trade up and down the Danish coast. She had two more owners before being bought in 2000 by Nikki Alford and given a new lease of life by restoring her to the graceful sailing ship she was over a hundred years ago. Today the *Bessie Ellen* is the last sailing boat from Braunton that is still working and can be hired for sailing holidays and educational trips and many other adventures in and around the coast of Devon and Cornwall.

Eileen Salter was born at 12, Station Road, the youngest of the six children of Bertie and Elizabeth Irwin. Bertie worked for Dick Symons who owned the sand barge *60 SPEC*. Eileen explained that in

John Squire Chichester, the first owner of the
Bessie Ellen *in 1906.*

Right: *Bessie Gould Chichester who carried on the shipping business after her husband's tragic accident at Sharpness lock.*

The ketch, Bessie Ellen.

those days the barges had to be loaded and unloaded by hand.

In 1936 when Eileen was only thirteen her father was involved in a terrible accident. It was February and Bertie Irwin left home for work at Vellator Quay at 8am. He told his wife that he was going to discharge his barge. An hour later the skipper Captain George Clarke was unable to find Bertie but as the hatches were open he knew that he had started work and assumed that Bertie had gone off to carry out another task.

Eileen continued the story by saying that when her father did not return home by 5pm her mother thought that he may have stopped off at his sister's house at Vellator to help her with some work. When Bertie still had not arrived much later she went to her neighbour and fellow seafarer William Mitchell and raised the alarm. William and his brother Frank informed the police and a search party was formed. Bertie's body was found at 3.15am the next morning when it was low tide. He was pinned under the bow of the barge but the body could only be released when the next tide came in and lifted the boat.

At the inquest it was found that he had not died from drowning but that death was due to shock from sudden immersion in cold water. A verdict of accidental death was returned by the jury with the advice that a rope should be attached to the barge that a man could hold on to if he found himself falling over the edge of the boat!

Eileen and Doreen Irwin outside 12, Station Road.

Chapter 7

A Village at Work

Butchers, Bakers and Sailmakers

Less than a century ago Braunton was almost completely self-supporting. There was a time when it could boast of being the largest village in the kingdom that could feed itself and also send produce to our towns and cities. Its beaches became the holiday playground for the rest of the country.

With no preferences made I've listed in alphabetical order some memories of the many trades that kept the parish of Braunton a thriving community.

Bakers

HOWARDS - Margaret Clarke, one of the daughters of the Church Street blacksmith, tells us that her grandfather William Howard and his family had a bakery and shop in Church Street. She says she loved to watch him and his son Will making loaves from the dough left to 'set' from the night before. He sometimes gave her a lump of it and she modelled animals which he baked in the enormous ovens.

Margaret also went on the delivery rounds with her Uncle William and as he was extremely shy it was she who had to get down from the horse driven van and go to the houses to see what was required.

This family business later moved to Caen Street (where Warren's Bakers are today) and was run by the Howard family until the late 1930s when it was sold to Alfred Kupke.

R. BUTLER & SON - After the Howards left Church Street, Ralph Butler, with his wife Ann and son Ron took over the bakery business. Ralph's granddaughter Geraldine told me that his father William Butler was a Master Grocer in Bideford and possibly a ship owner who traded with Ireland. William and Ann had seven children and when William died Ann carried on the business

Ralph Butler born 1879.
Baker in Church Street.

Ellen Butler married to Ralph Butler.
She ran a grocer's shop beside the bakery.

until she died and Ralph inherited it. It was then that Ralph and his family moved to Braunton and became R. Butler & Son.

A daughter, Dorothy, was born 1920 whilst they were living in Church Street and she told her daughter Geraldine that her father and brother Ron started work at 5.30am to have the bread ready for the early morning customers. There was a second baking in the afternoon. Saturday was especially busy which meant the whole family had to help out. Dorothy attended a private school in the Congregational Rooms in East Street until she was fourteen then had to stay at home to help her mother.

In 1926 they moved the business to behind St Brannock's church (today the house is called Baker's Thatch). The bakehouse was behind the house up a lane beside the New Inn. The family lived there until 1962.

Baker's Thatch where the Butlers ran their bakery and grocery business.

MOON & SONS – Frederick Watts Moon learnt his trade at Lake's Bakery in Caen Street, next to the railway station. In 1895 he opened his own bakery at West Cross at the bottom of North Street and lived over the shop

Frederick Watts Moon's motorised van which he ran from his shop at West Cross.

with his wife and three sons, Leslie, Wilfred and Archie.

The shop became more than just a bakery as they were soon advertising that they were 'speciality bakers, confectioners, grocers and corn merchants' and when their father died in 1948, Wilfred remained the baker and Leslie concentrated on the grocery side of the business. Archie had become a teacher.

Wilfred later moved to Knowle and took over the post office and village store and in 1960 Leslie had the shop at West Cross redesigned and enlarged and it became an up-market delicatessen and coffee shop.

A.J. KUPKE – In 1936 Alfred Kupke married Winifred Venner of the Post Office at Filleigh. Soon after, they bought Howard's bakers shop and bakehouse in Caen Street, with accommodation. They moved in on the Saturday and opened the shop on Monday morning with their own freshly baked bread. Winifred's nephew Norman Venner reminisces about the time he spent with his aunt and uncle.

Norman and his six siblings lived with their parents on a small farm on the edge of Exmoor.

When he was three he was seriously ill in hospital with peritonitis and Norman very nearly died. Whilst he was recovering it was recommended by the doctors that he should move to be near the sea to help with his recovery.

Uncle Alfred and Aunt Winifred did not have any children and so it was decided that Norman should live with them to get the sea air. Norman's elder brother Robert came to keep him company. Later his small sister Thelma came too. Norman remembers with great sadness that Thelma died at the age of seven from meningitis. When he went into her bedroom to see her she gave him her two most precious toys to look after, a black racing horse and an African chief, which he says he still has to this day.

At the back of the shop was the bakehouse with its large ovens. His uncle could never be out any later than 9pm as he had to stoke the coke fires to ensure that they were at the right temperature for the bakers when they came to work at 5am. Louie Bozinni who made the cakes later became a head patissier at a top London Hotel.

Norman said his uncle would not permit any of his nephews into the shop when it was open. However, if Norman disobeyed this rule one of the shop assistants, Gladys Watt, would wrap her apron around him if they heard Mr Kupke coming into the shop. But it wasn't all bad for Norman as he was allowed to help make the doughnuts each morning by sugaring

them and putting the jam inside. He would then have two hot ones for his breakfast!

Next door to the baker's was George Chugg's newsagents and next to that was an accountant's. When George Chugg moved his business to where Braunton Newsagents are today Winifred Kupke bought the shop next door and opened it as a Woolcraft shop and sometime later she also purchased the accountant's and extended the business.

When the boys reached eleven they went to Shebbear College and when term time finished they would return to Braunton for a couple of days before going back to their parents' farm.

In 1955 when the Kupkes retired they sold the bakery business to North Devon Bakery and they moved to Stockwell Lodge in South Street.

Uncle Alfred died in 1960 and Aunty Winifred was remarried in 1965/6 to Alfred Dennis. Alfred who originated from Knowle, had emigrated to Australia with just his bag of carpenter's tools. He was on a return visit to the old country after his wife died. On a sightseeing coach trip he found an empty seat next to Winifred Kupke. Before he returned to Australia he had asked her to marry him and bought her a return ticket just in case she didn't like it when she got out there. However, once there they married and had eight years of happiness. As they both had had partners with the same names not to confuse their relatives in Australia and Braunton Alf Dennis was referred as Rex in this country and Winifred was called Freda in Australia!

Nancy Barnes and Kupke's bakery van in Exeter Road in 1945.

Before we leave Kupke's Bakery we must tell the story of how Nancy Barnes met her husband Thomas. When Nancy's parents died in 1940 she decided it was time to go into the wide world outside. She learnt to drive and spent the rest of the war years delivering bread and cakes for Kupke's Bakery to outlying villages and RAF Chivenor.

One day during her rounds Nancy met Thomas Barnes who came from North Buckland. Although she had seen Tom around at dances and concerts, on this occasion she had lost her baker's basket from the back of the van. She asked Tom if on his travels he found it, would he take it back to the shop? He did find it and returned it. In days past ladies just used to drop their handkerchief to catch a gentleman's attention. A baker's basket is different – but with the same result!

They married in 1946 and had three children, seven grandchildren and eight great-grandchildren. Tom died in 1987. At ninety-six years old Nancy is still living at North Buckland near her family and with a memory sharp enough to help me with many stories in this book!

Blacksmith

ELLIOTT – Margaret Clarke's father John Elliott was the blacksmith at the bottom of Church Street in the 1890s. She said it was terrifying to see him trying to master a young horse just in from the fields and being shod for the first time. Sometimes he put a hood on the horse so it could not see the fire, but he had lots of kicks which injured his legs and caused him suffering in later life. After the South African War, horse shoes were factory made and the only work left to do was nail on the shoes after paring the hooves. With blacksmithing in such a poor way her father decided to take on the licence of the Black Horse Inn opposite their home. However, he kept the smithy-

John A Elliott – Blacksmith and licensee of the Black Horse Inn in Church Street. Assistant blacksmith Bill Barrow shoeing the horse and John (Jocker) Smith who married Rose – read her story in the 'In Service' item of this chapter.

ing going all the time they lived at the public house and only gave up both businesses when his wife died shortly after WWI when the whole country was hit by an epidemic of influenza.

Butchers' Shops in Braunton

W.T. Ellis East Street – A. Dennis and Son bottom Heanton Street – Jack Reed South Street – C.H. Ellis South Street and Meadow Fresh opposite the railway station.

REED'S – at the end of South Street is the only butchers left in Braunton in the 21st century and it remains the longest serving butcher's shop in the village. The original butchers were the Drake family who had owned the business since 1777.

Tony Reed's grandfather Claudius Alfred Reed was married to Louise who also came from a Braunton butchering family, the Isaacs, who owned a shop on the Square at the end of East Street. Louise ran the shop with the help of her son Jack (Tony's father). Claude kept stables behind the shop from where he hired out his horses for riding as well as for working in the fields and on farms.

In the 1930s there were five butcher's shops in the village – Reed's, Ellis, Dennis (two brothers Phillip and Arthur) and Isaac's.

Basket Makers

Mr Mock at work in the Basket Factory at the top of Heanton Street.

Right: *Basket makers outside the Basket Factory.*

Reed's Butcher's shop as it was originally.

Leaving school in 1954 at fifteen, Tony joined the family business. In 1960 he was placed third in a competition as Butcher's Apprentice of the Year and in 1961 his father made him a partner.

In 1968 they entered an international competition in France and won a gold medal for their black puddings and the following year the bronze prize. After this the business has had success after success in competitions with their sausages and pies.

Tony has now retired and left his son Russell in charge of the butcher's block.

Tony and Russell Reed with the silver trophy they won in October 2013 for their sausages.

Tony Reed's grandfather Claudius Alfred Reed who used to lead the Barnstaple Carnival. Seen here in Rock Park before the parade started.

ELLIS BUTCHERS – Brian Ellis's grandparents had a farm at Bucks Mills where they brought up four sons: Jim, William Thomas (known as Tom), Charles Henry (known as Harry) and Bert.

Being the eldest son, Jim took over the farm and Bert joined the Great Western Railway.

Tom went to Braunton and worked for a while driving a car for the local doctor. He later opened a butcher's shop, W.T. Ellis, on the Square.

Brian's father Harry with his wife Ethel and family lived at 16, South Street and Harry opened his own butchers shop there, C.H. Ellis. In the evenings he also operated a fish and chip business from the premises next door.

Brian remembers that next to the fish and chip shop was Mrs Lee's grocery shop, then Mr Dendle's café which during the war was taken over by the NAAFI as a canteen.

Brian's mother died when he was only ten and as his brother and sister were older than him and already going to Barnstaple Grammar School he found that he was doing a lot of the chores at home and even preparing their school lunches before they rushed off to catch the train in the mornings.

A job he loved to do was deliver the mince-meat and corned beef to Kupke's the baker in Caen Street. If he got there before 7am he was rewarded by being allowed to fill his own doughnuts with jam and roll them in sugar.

When Brian left school he went straight to work in his father's butchers although he really wanted to go to sea. While he was at school he had worked at weekends and holidays. However, his father had always let him have one week off during the school summer holidays and he would go to sea with either Alf Parkhouse in the *Clara May* or Bill Mitchell and his father in the *Agnes* or Captain Coates in the *Democrat*.

One of Brian's interests over the years has been his lurcher dogs and rabbiting with them. He used to rent farm land at Knowle and one night caught 98 rabbits. This was not only sport but also business as during the 1940s and '50s rabbit was a cheap and wholesome meal. Many, many rabbits caught in the Devonshire countryside were sent to London by train every day to feed those in the city who could not get much meat. (Rationing meant that one person was allowed 1/9d worth of meat a week and 10d worth of corned beef.)

One day Brian's friend said he was going to Exeter greyhound racing and as he had seen how Brian's dog Misty could run could he take her with him and test her against the greyhounds. Brian said Misty would catch the dummy hare. 'Oh no! she's not that fast' said his friend. Misty was lined up with the rest and when the gates on the cage went up the other dogs tore off in pursuit of the hare but Misty cut across the tracks and sat waiting for the hare to come around the corner of the track and then caught it by the neck! A case of more brains than brawn!

Brian met his wife Pauline at a dance in the Pavillion Ilfracombe one Saturday night and they married and moved into 16 South Street with his father. When Arthur Dennis the butcher at Heanton Street retired Brian took over his shop but kept the Dennis name.

Later he bought the first shop to be built in the Caen Shopping Parade. He moved from the Square and his customers moved with him and when he first opened they had to clamber over builder's boards to get through his shop door!

His father Harry and Tom worked together and sold the East Street shop and opened a larger shop at the bottom of Heanton Street. They also had two mobile shops and whilst meat rationing was still on sold fish from one of the vans but later meat was sold from both. They opened a butcher's shop at Croyde and employed ex-servicemen.

Brian said not to forget that the butchers in Braunton used to slaughter their own animals in their own small slaughter houses. They were in Sings Lane, Chaloners Road, Dennis's had one behind their shop which today is the car park behind Webber's the Estate Agents and Reed's had one behind their shop. Later a purpose built slaughterhouse was built in Chapple Street.

Cattle Transporters

John Watts, Founder of J. Watts & Sons, Cattle Transporters bought the business in 1925 from Mr Geen, a grocer on the Square in Braunton. The sale included a horse and wagon. John was only a young man but he was soon purchasing his first lorry.

John and his wife Hannah had 12 children: six girls and six boys and they lived at Hordens Farm in South Street. Three of his sons went into the business with him – Stanley, Norman and Reginald.

They would transport almost anything from coal from the railway station to bulbs from the Bulb Farm and seaweed from Lee beach taken back to the Bulb Farm to be used as manure.

Mr Symonds of Croyde bought sheep and ponies from Lundy Island and then had them shipped to Instow. From there Watts collected them and took them to Barnstaple Cattle Market for sale on a Friday.

Ellis the Butchers at the bottom of Heanton Street.

One of John Watts first lorries with four of his 12 children. L-R: Gladys, Ruth and Roy. Reg is at the wheel.

John Watts in later years.

Picnicking at Crow lighthouse.

Reg Watts loads pigs into his lorry at Barnstaple Cattle Market.

Reg's wife Ruth remembers that Crow lighthouse light was fuelled by bottle gas which J. Watts and Sons supplied. They would lay straw bales on the back of the lorry and as a family would go out to Crow Point and have a picnic when they were delivering the gas.

Harold Moon was also a haulier among his other business enterprises. He was in WWI but was too ill to go to the front so served the war as a farrier. Later he was a turf accountant and a haulier. He had a horse and cart and would collect and deliver any commodity. One of his jobs was to row a dinghy full of coal out to the hospital isolation ship moored in the estuary.

Cobbler

Bertie Buckingham outside his cobbler's in South Street. Recalled by all who knew him as a friendly character who worked amongst a muddle of his tools and the boots and shoes he had to repair and his cats! He always made time to stop and talk to everyone who passed his house.

Cordwainer

William Alfred Reed was a cordwainer (shoemaker) who lived with his wife Ellen and five children at 17, Church Street. His great grandson Douglas Reed said that William worked in a little wooden shed at the back of their house. He was also a part-time postman, delivering post twice a day around the village and returning to his shoemaking between rounds.

Cordwainer (shoemaker) William Reed of 17, Church Street. He had a workshop at the back of the house.

Cycle Factory

Brothers John and Richard Prior who lived with their parents Pip and Audrey at the London Inn during the 1940s, said their father owned a cycle factory beside the railway line between Braunton Station and Georgeham Crossing. They were manufacturering trade bicycles such as butchers and bakers used for delivering their goods. These were mostly for export to India. Once made the bikes were crated up and sent away by train.

Florence and John Clarke at Knowle where they started their dairy.

Dairy

In the 1930s there were three dairies in Braunton – Leonard Chugg's dairy, the Station Dairies run by Mr. Pook (where Cawthorne's is today) and Clarke's. John Clarke's grandparents John and Florence ran a campsite at Knowle as well as a dairy and from there they delivered milk around the area. When the new road was cut through Braunton they moved their dairy business to a shop in Exeter Road, in 1937. One side of the shop sold dairy goods and on the other side was a café. The actual dairy was out the back of the shop.

In that same year their son Reginald married Florence whom he had met at a dance at the Parish Hall. She was in service at Hillsview and Reginald was a milkman for the family business

John's grandparents John and Florence lived above the shop in Exeter Road along with their daughter Phyllis and her husband Frederick Woodley who worked on the railway at Braunton Station.

Grandfather John was head of the business and was also a gamekeeper at Buckland House for the Incledon-Webbers. When WWII broke out grandfather gave up his gamekeeping and ran the dairy full-time as Reg went to war in the Army Catering Corp.

John Clarke with his daughter Phyllis and two friends.

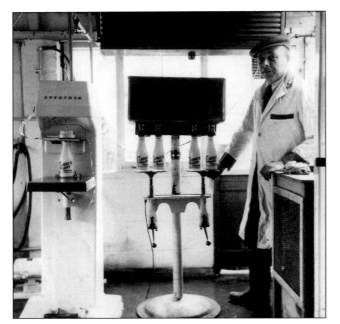

Reg Clarke at work bottling milk at their Exeter Road Dairy.

With Fred and Reg away in the Army Phyllis ran the shop and café which was popular with servicemen billeted in and around Braunton as well as all the American soldiers who were under canvass alongside the Saunton Road.

Returning to John's story, he said that before he left school he had to work as a delivery roundsman at weekends and in the summer the workload trebled as they delivered bottles of milk to campsites in the area. This meant delivering to each tent and caravan and not just leaving the milk in bulk at the camp shop. There was never a day off, not even Christmas Day, although one year they did two deliveries on Christmas Eve and were so exhausted by packing two days' work into one that they all

Frederick Woodley and Phyllis Clarke marry in 1940.

slept through the Christmas festivities!

John says although he didn't feel that he was cut out to work in the business the job did have some good points for a young teenage lad. There was a Captain Hunt, who lived on Wrafton Road, and he would leave his front door unlocked, the money on the table and instructions that John could make himself a cup of tea. This was good news for John, especially on Sundays, as he would settle down for a few stolen moments of tea, biscuits and the titillation of the *News of the World's* Pin Up girls!

After leaving school John worked full-time in the business but his father knew that his heart wasn't in the job and when he heard of a clerical post at RAF Chivenor he told John to apply for it. So in 1955 John started his long career in the Civil Service.

When John Clarke Senior died in 1954 his son Reg took over the dairy, they sold the shop in Exeter Road and moved to Chaloner's Road. In 1964 Clarke's Dairy was sold to Mr Frisby.

Drapers

Nellie and Winnie Chichester (the daughters of mariner Capt. John Chichester) had a draper's and haberdasher's shop at 5, Caen Street. They lived over the shop until they married.

Dress Shops

In the first half of the twentieth century it was usual for clothes to be hand-made, either at home, or for the more wealthy, by a tailoress or dressmaker.

But, after WWII mass production meant there was a wider choice at reasonable cost and dress shops became the pleasure of all fashion-conscious women. However, this explosion of mass-produced garments meant that you were very likely to arrive at a social occasion, such as a dance at the Braunton's Parish Hall, only to find the copy of your haute couture number being worn by another young lady also trying to look their most chic!

Braunton was not left behind in the ladies' fashion stakes especially in the 1950s and '60s when cocktail dresses and long evening gowns were always worn to anything from the village dance to banquets and Hunt Balls. A name that springs to mind here is Mrs Rene Kingdom who was a high class milliner and dress maker and owned a dress shop in the village. She also designed and dressed the Carnival Queens and attendants for both Barnstaple and Braunton for many years.

Christine Braund remembers working in Joan's Dress Shop in East Street. Joan and Ted Butler owned the shop along with another they had in Croyde.

Joan's sold mens, womens and childrens fashions, schoolwear, swimwear, shoes, hats, gloves and scarves. But Joan would never put anything into a sale, so clothes stayed in the shop, and just moved further back each year until they ended up in the stock room.

Occasionally when business was slack Christine and another sales assistant would have a turnout but Joan would be very reluctant to actually get rid of anything. One day when the boss wasn't around the two women decided to have a go at sorting out the back room. When they came across a pair of winkle-picker stiletto boots crumpled and covered in mildrew they decided these just had to go. They wrapped them in paper and threw them into the rubbish bin for the next day's collection. You can imagine their horror when the women arrived for work the next day and found the boots in the middle of the road where the dustmen had dropped them when emptying the bin! These boots that were not made for walking found their way into a bonfire!

BRAUNTON ELECTRIC LIGHT AND POWER CO. LTD. This was owned by ship owner Henry Clarke. His brother-in-law James Welch who had been a wheelwright at Simonsbath moved with his wife Elizabeth to Braunton and became the electrical engineer for the Electric Light Company.

In March 1912 they were connecting those houses in the village that wanted and could afford this new-fangled way of illumination. Electric street lighting was first used in this country in 1881 but wasn't in general use throughout the country until 1921.

Gift Shop

We have to produce gifts for holidaymakers for them to remember us by and to this end Braunton has done its best to fill that need. Today the village has several shops that stock all the best Devon can produce – some useful, some attractive and others just delicious to eat!

James Thomas Welch on the right. A wheelwright at Simonsbath, he came to Braunton to become the engineer at Electric Light and Power Company.

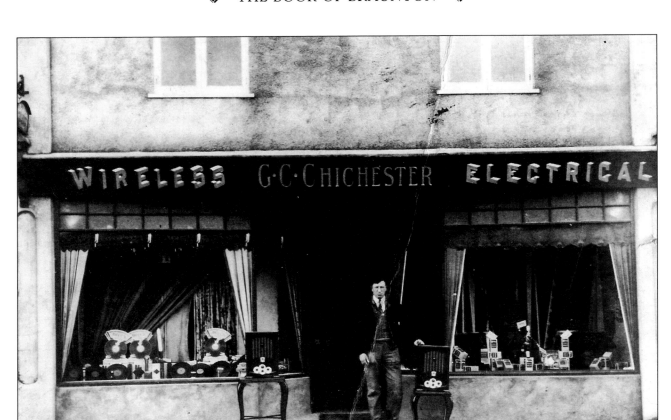

George Chichester outside his electrical shop in Exeter Road. He had the shop built in his parents' South Street back garden in preparation for the Exeter Road being opened.

Joan Incledon and her husband John, who was a well-known character in the village, worked for Elma Williams for ten years in her shop in the Square at the bottom of East Street. It was named 'Devon Made' because everything they sold was made in Devon – Brannam Pottery as well as other local pottery, patchwork quilts made in Clovelly and many other forms of art work; Dartington clothes, Saunders of Barnstaple sheepskin goods and wooden toys. John also made furniture for the shop, stools and small tables which he also sold at Barnstaple Market.

Grocers

BRADLEY'S GROCERS – Florence Chapple of the Brookside Stores and Post Office at Knowle worked at Braunton Telephone Exchange. Florence met and married Frederick Bradley in 1943 and together they owned and ran Bradley's Grocery Shop in East Street.

CRANCH'S – Gerald Cranch had been working as a fishmonger in Kingsbridge when with his wife Muriel they decided to begin a new life in Braunton. It was 1954 and their eldest daughter Hettie was eleven and youngest daughter Jean was seven. In Braunton they had bought Hill's General Store at 1 Church Street and renamed it Cranch's.

Jean remembers they had a very large back garden that went right down to the churchyard of St Bran-

nock's. They had three greenhouses and kept chickens. There was also a railway carriage from the Lynton to Barnstaple Railway in the garden where Jean and her friend Yvonne Irwin used to play house

All the family played a role in the business and Jean's job was to feed their chickens. She said many people kept chickens and sometimes a pig in their back gardens. Gerald Cranch would buy their eggs

Fred and Florence (Flo) Bradley outside their grocer's shop in East Street.

Colling's grocery shop in the Square where Marsdens is today. They won first prize with this window display.

and it was Jean's job to put them in trays ready for the Egg Marketing Board man to collect them on a Thursday. She was paid one old penny for every tray she filled!

Thursdays and Fridays were busy times for Gerald and Muriel as Gerald did a country round in his van and on a Thursday went out and around the villages and collected his orders. Jean said he would come back with a host of scraps of paper with people's shopping lists. The family spent the whole evening putting the orders together in time for Gerald to set off early next morning to deliver them – long before supermarkets came up with the idea!

While Muriel took care of the shop Gerald would go into Barnstaple and collect the supplies including poultry and animal feed from Rolle Quay.

Jean especially remembers Beryl Watts who worked for them in the shop for eighteen years and continued working for the next owners after Gerald and Muriel left in 1973.

In Service

This job title is rarely used any more but up until the 1950s it was a position for many a young girl and usually meant living in at their place of work.

Joan Incledon was the third of seven children when in 1937 they came to Chivenor for her father to work at Heanton Court Farm. In 1940 the family moved to East Street, Braunton, to work for Bill Lane at Broadgate Farm.

At Braunton Senior School Joan especially enjoyed Domestic Science. This led to her first job in 1940 in service as a 'tweenie' (this is a maid who works below stairs in the kitchens as well as upstairs) at a large house overlooking Saunton Beach belonging to Mr and Mrs Lycett who were steel magnates. When she was first in the job Joan only had half a day off a week and the family let her borrow a bicycle to ride home to Chivenor. Joan later became independent when she bought her sister Freda's bike from her for £1.10s (£1. 50p).

In 1941 Joan went to work for a war-time RAF Officer in Lower Park Road and soon afterwards she found a placement in the household of Mr Jonas, a surgeon. There was a cook here and Joan was the housemaid responsible for cleaning, fires and fetching coal. Once again she only had half a day a week off.

In 1944 Joan at eighteen decided it was time to do her bit for the war effort and went to work in the carpenters' shop at Chivenor.

Dorothy Davies' first job was to help look after the family of Mr and Mrs Williams who lived over their men's outfitters shop in the Square. It was her job to look after the two children, Elma and Brian and to help with the housework. The shop was double fronted and Mrs Williams's brother and sister had the other side as a shoe shop.

Another of Dot's jobs was at Heanton Court where her role was one of housemaid. The house was owned by Mr Dunn, a bachelor, who was looked after by a housekeeper Miss Barnes and a cook Gertie Tozer.

Among her memories was the open fireplace in the kitchen where the whole part of a tree trunk was placed in the fireplace and set alight and as it burned so the rest of the trunk was pushed into the fire.

Joan Incledon on the right of the group, at Broadgate Farm, East Street.

The tree trunk that was slowly fed into the kitchen fire at Heanton Court.

57

There were also faggots made of a bundle of Ash sticks – these were burned until clinkers, which heated the oven and cooked the food. Dot especially remembers the cook's wonderful apple dumplings.

Michael Butcher sent me this story from his home in Australia, of his great grandmother Rose who was born in Paris sometime before 29 August 1887.

Rose was cared for and educated in an English orphanage. It was at the orphanage that she met and formed a lifelong relationship with Dame Clara Butt, the famous opera singer. Clara was a major benefactor of the orphanage and visited regularly when in Paris.

According to Rose's daughter Eleanor (known as Maidy) Rose's father visited her regularly, taking her out to lunch and making payments towards her care and education. However, he did not keep in touch once Rose started work.

In 1901 Rose was nineteen and working as an under housemaid for the wealthy merchant family of Henry Millar in Hampstead, London.

By 1904 she had entered the employ of Edward and Augusta Lloyd as a nursery governess to their two children when they moved back from Paris to Hampstead. Soon afterwards they moved to Sylvester House, Silver Street, Braunton and Rose went with them. Rose was probably with this family for three or four years before meeting and marrying John

Rose Passmore.

Passmore (as seen in the photograph of John Elliott the blacksmith) at St Brannock's church on 12 March, 1908.

Michael says that Rose must have had a close relationship with the Lloyd family as Mrs Lloyd paid for Rose's wedding and was one of the witnesses at her wedding to John.

After the marriage Rose and John lived at Kittiwell, Knowle and subsequently in the School House, Caen Street. She had eight children and spent the rest of her life in Braunton where she died in 1955 aged seventy-three.

Rose's friendship with Clara Butt was sufficiently strong for Dame Clara to visit Rose from time to time, staying in South Street, Braunton.

Ironmongers

SLEE'S HOME HARDWARE – Up until 1922 the site in the Square at the end of Caen Street had been a farm. Alison Serret's great grandfather Harry Slee, who was a builder, demolished the farm and built two shops – the first one was an ironmongers for his son Frank and next door was for Frank's cousins Escott and Herbert Scoins to run as a gentlemen's outfitters.

In 1929 Frank Slee and his wife Irene became the proud and surprised parents of triplets. They were born over the shop – Peter, John and Elizabeth (known always as Betty).

The Square looking towards the farm that was demolished in Caen Street to make way for Slee's ironmonger's shop in 1922.

Slee's shop on the left in a very quiet Caen Street.

Peter and John joined their father in the business, John specializing as an electrician and he also took on apprentices and trained them. Peter worked with his father in the ironmonger's side of the shop.

Betty wanted a nursing career and trained as a midwife in Barnstaple. She married Sven Hylder-gaard and had two children. The family emigrated to Canada in the late 1970s.

Peter met Margaret Alford, a primary school teacher, when she came to Braunton to take up a position at Caen Street School. Their only daughter Alison was born in 1963 and went to South Mead School just as it opened. Then to Braunton School and Community College (today Braunton Academy) and on to North Devon College (today Petroc) where she learnt all the attributes for being a secretary at Webber's Estate Agents in the Square, Braunton.

Some years later Alison followed her dream of becoming a nursery school teacher. After training she opened her own nursery school in her home in South Street which she ran for eleven years.

Alison's husband Gary had joined Slee's family business in 1993 and in 1998 Alison joined as well.

HOME HARDWARE A DEALER OWNED WHOLESALE COMPANY – In 1961 a group of local retailers from Braunton, Barnstaple, Bideford, and Ilfracombe got together and bought Barnfords a Bideford wholesale company. They became a co-operative and called it Home Hardware South West. They soon outgrew the Bideford warehouse and moved into the recently vacated Ford and Lock warehouse at Vellator.

This was the first Home Hardware business. There are now 400 throughout England and Wales.

Every member pays into the company and has shares in it. The company has buyers who buy in the products – saltcellars to snow shovels! It's good to know that from one small acorn planted in Braunton

this enterprise has grown into one relatively large oak tree that has spread its branches all over the country.

Men's Outfitters

C.H. WILLIAMS GENTLEMEN'S TAILORS AND OUTFITTERS – Retired Schoolmaster Brian Williams explained that in 1916, when WWI broke out, his father Charles, who was a devout Christian became a Conscientious Objector and was sent to gaol. Here he got a good education as there were many educated and professional men in prison with him.

Before the war Charles had trained as a tailor under William Manaton at his shop in Church Street.

In 1924 Charles married Amy Tossell whose father owned Tossell's Boot and Shoe Emporium on the Square.

Brian's aunt Lily and uncle Arthur bought the Grocery Shop (now Marsdens) and ran it as a shoe shop while Charles and Amy ran his grandfather's shop as the tailors and outfitters.

After Charles Williams died in 1973 Brian's sister Elma changed the outfitting business into one of selling goods only made in Devon and aptly named 'Devon Made'.

Williams the men's outfitters and Tossell's shoe shop are behind the traffic lights. Brian Williams whose bedroom was at the front of the building used to watch an owl that roosted in the Cross Tree right outside his bedroom. He cried when the tree was felled because the owl would no longer have a home but a kindly policeman explained that they were going to replace the tree with a traffic light so the owl could sit on that! R.L. Knight

Postmen and Telephonist

David Fry was brought up at Knowle at the Brookside Stores and Post Office which his father Edmund and mother Annie had taken over from her sisters Jane and Florence. Florence worked at Braunton Telephone Exchange which was over the Post Office in Caen Street.

When Edmund and Annie moved into the Knowle shop Annie ran that business and Edmund worked as a postman in Braunton and was also cleaner of the

David Fry with his parents Edmund and Annie outside Brookside Stores, Knowle.

The 'Hello Girls' telephonists at Braunton Telephone Exchange. On the left Betty Balsh and on the right Flo Chapple who later married Fred Bradley and they had a grocers in East Street.

Edmund and Annie Fry.

Royal Mail staff from the Caen Street Post Office.

David Fry as a police cadet outside the Brookside Stores.

Barbara Goodliffe (on the left) was the only postwoman in Braunton between 1959 and 1978. Seen here with Mrs Remington when her husband retired as a postman.

telephone exchange. David recalls how his father and aunt would cycle to work in Braunton very early in the morning and when his father returned to Knowle in the afternoon he would set to and help his wife in the shop and post office.

David said his father cycled everywhere on his rounds even to the lighthouse at Crow Point to deliver the post office mail and Trinity House mail. At times in the summer his father would take David on the cross bar of his bicycle out to the lighthouse where sometimes they had tea with the keeper and his family. Other more dangerous times were when the American servicemen were training with live ammunition on the Burrows and he found he was caught in the cross fire. Even in the worst of the winter the mail had to be delivered. On occasions, when it was thick snow, Edmund found himself cycling off the road and into the drainage dyke on Braunton Marsh!

Edmund's life ended tragically when he was killed in an early morning road accident when cycling at Heddon's Mill, Knowle, in December 1956. He had been delivering newspapers when he was hit by a car. His son David, who had just finished his national service and was returning to the Devon Constabulary as a policeman, was soon on the scene and went with his father to the hospital, where he died three hours later.

Some of the telephonists – 2nd from left, Jean Mullen, 4th Wendy Saunders, 6th supervisor Betty Peart and (second from right) Anne Zambuni.

system came into action, nobody in Braunton had dialling phones. To make a call they had to lift the receiver and call the operator. It was an extremely busy switchboard which had five positions which were covered twenty-four hours a day.

Potter – Fred Luscombe

Marie Ash told me her mother Doris's story - She was the seventh of eight children when her mother died of TB. As her father could not manage with all his young family five year old Doris was sent to Braunton to live with an aunt and uncle – Lucy and Fred Luscombe.

Fred was a potter at Braunton Pottery in Station Road which with his partner Harry Chichester they bought in 1962.

After leaving school Doris worked as a doctor's receptionist in the village and then married Roy Lucas who was a National Serviceman serving at RAF Chivenor. Later Doris, Roy and their two children Marie and Neil moved back to Braunton to help Fred look after Lucy, who was very ill.

Marie remembers Uncle Fred as a 'Gentle Giant'. He had such huge hands and it always amazed Marie that he

Braunton's switchboard on its last day of operation in 1971.

Wendy Saunders worked as a telephonist at Braunton from 1965 to 1971 when the manual Telephone Exchange moved from above the post office in Caen Street to a new Digital Exchange at the rear of the car park in Exeter Road.

Wendy explained that before the new digital

Doris in the garden of Pear Tree Cottage.

Fred Luscombe throwing a pot at the Braunton Pottery in 1964.

could make such delicate works of art. He told her that he had worked at many trades, a butcher, baker and a candlestick maker! He had worked as a butcher's boy for Dennis' the Butchers in the Square where he earned 1s 6d (7 ½p) a week and his food.

On Saturday afternoons he would settle down in his chair to watch wrestling. Marie remembers he smoked a large pipe and when he got excited over the shenanigans on the TV he would shout at the screen, which would send up a shower of sparks from his pipe, many of them landing on his armchair, leaving permanent reminders of his Saturday afternoon's pleasure!

Public Houses

THE RED LION

John Phillips was born ten minutes before Christmas Day in 1930 at Miss Maynes Nursing Home in East Street. His grandfather Thomas White was the licensee of the public house, The Red Lion which stood in the Square at the end of Caen Street. John and his mother who was the daughter of Mr and Mrs White only remained in Braunton for a short while before joining his father in Woolacombe where he remained for many years. However, now retired he has returned with his wife to his roots in Braunton.

The Red Lion had to make way for progress when Chaloners Road was cut through into the Square.

At work in the pottery in Station Road.

The Red Lion at the end of Caen Street on the Square. It was demolished to make way for the new Barnstaple to Ilfracombe road through the village. John Phillips' grandfather Thomas White was landlord here in 1907.

LONDON INN

John Prior was revisiting his childhood home in Braunton when he told me how his parents Pip and Audrey Prior took over the licence of the London Inn in Caen Street in 1939. They had previously lived at Penzance where Audrey had given birth to twin boys, Richard and Martin in 1938. Sadly Martin only lived for a short while and this was the reason they moved to North Devon.

In a telephone call later Richard Prior told me that the family ran the London Inn with the help of Mrs Sellers. Her husband had a shoe repairers shop next door to the pub. With Mrs Sellers working hard behind the scenes it allowed Audrey Prior to work as a teacher across the road at Caen Street School. Later she taught at Heanton Primary School.

John was born in the nursing home in Wrafton Road in 1943 and the brothers have good memories of the time they lived in Braunton. They both recall the large mural that was painted on the wall in the bar and such characters as author Negley Farson who lived on the edge of Putsborough Sands and entertained everyone with his tales of past times. Richard said he was a great man who wrote books on fly fishing.

The family moved to Sidmouth in 1950.

MARINERS ARMS

Nancy Skinner's grandfather John Ridge came from The Plough Inn, Bickington to take over the licence of the Mariners Arms in South Street and his wife Ellen made a grocery shop out of one half of the premises. They had six children – Harry, Jack, Alfred, Nell, Ada and Ernest (Nancy's father Bill).

When John died in 1923 his eldest son Harry took over the licence. Harry remained a bachelor and his sister Ada lived at the pub and looked after him even after she married Mr Abbott and they had two daughters.

Jack and Alfred both became tailors and one moved to Wales and the other to Oxford.

During Harry's reign at the Mariners it was solely a men's pub – mainly fishermen and seafaring folk. Nancy said that her Uncle Harry had strong views

The Railway Hotel at the bottom of Heanton Street. This was demolished when the Exeter Road was built and the George Hotel was built on the opposite side of the road.

about women not being made welcome in his establishment – it was a men only domain where ale was consumed and skittles, darts and cribbage were played. There was only one exception and that was an elderly woman who would knock on the hatch window in the passage to the bar and ask for "a glass please Harry". He would pour her a glass of Guinness, shut the hatch and leave her to drink her beer in the hallway. The drink consumed, she would soon be on her way up the street.

Youngest of the family, Bill had been in the Navy for twenty-two years when he met his wife Chris at Beer in East Devon when they were both visiting friends. They married at St Brannock's church in 1923.

The Rev. Prince married them at 8am one morning as he had to catch the 9am train to London! The only guests, at this unholy hour were the bridegroom's sister Ada and his best friend Jimmy Dunn who lived in East Street.

After their marriage Bill and Chris lived in East Street and Bill, a Chief Petty Officer, left the Navy. After trying several jobs he joined the Coastguard Service in 1930 and they moved to Bwlchtocyn in North Wales where Nancy was born.

Bill and Chris Ridge.

In 1938 when Nancy was seven years old Bill was posted to Port Isaac on the North Cornish coast. Nancy remembers her childhood in Cornwall with great pleasure although she also recalls some of the pranks her brother John got up to. On one occasion he put her into the black cone that her father would hoist up the flagpole to let fishermen at sea know that bad weather was approaching and that they should return to harbour. John hoisted the cone with Nancy inside up the flag pole and it was only her loud protestations that brought her help.

In 1946 when Nancy was fifteen her Uncle Harry died and her father left the Coastguard Service and returned to Braunton to take over the Mariners Arms. Bill and Chris ran the pub between them until 1954 when they retired. Nancy recalls that her mother always ran the pub on her own on Fridays as everyone went to Barnstaple for Market Day when the pubs stayed open all day.

For a couple of years before they retired Bill held a fruit and flower show in the pub's skittle alley which proved to be very popular.

Rabbit Dealer – Kathleen Harris

Kathleen's father, Thomas Braunton, was a rabbit catcher and originally from Tawstock. He would rent fields on a farm and have sole rights to catch and sell the rabbits. As he was limited on his land use he soon broadened his business by buying rabbits from other trappers and so became a wholesaler.

Before long he was collecting from Barnstaple, Braunton, West Down, Ashford, Pippacott and Nethercott.

This proved to be a successful business and helped Thomas to build up land he owned to form his own farm – Greenhill at Middle Marwood.

Kathleen was now given the job of collecting the rabbits from around the countryside. These would be left at the end of the farm lane in the hedge. Kathleen would leave the payment for the rabbits in a tin box. She had a tight schedule as she had to make the afternoon train every weekday from Braunton Station where she would send a thousand rabbits tied in pairs in wicker baskets to Smithfield Market. Forty were packed into each hamper and then weighed and charged by the weight of the hamper. Kathleen said she hated the smell of the rabbits and was always glad when the porters packed them for her. She would give them a rabbit in payment for which they were very grateful as it would make good eating for a family – although she could never bring herself to eat a meal made with rabbit.

Kathleen Harris (left) *with her dogs on the farm and* (above) *with the van she used to collect the rabbits from farms and scrap metal during wartime.*

A smelly business, but she adds that it was also very lucrative as the profits helped buy her first marital home. She added that there was only two rabbit wholesalers in North Devon during the war years – herself and Percy Brend who went on to open his own butchers business in Barnstaple and later a chain of West Country hotels.

Although petrol was rationed during the war years Kathleen was given a fuel allowance to run her little delivery van as it was seen by the authorities that her work was helping to feed the nation. And to help the war effort even further she would collect scrap metal from the villages of Marwood parish. Due to the shortage of fuel which led to very few private vehicles on the roads, and only one country bus a week, Kathleen would find herself helping out her customers by delivering their groceries or feed stuffs from Braunton or on occasions even taking people to hospital.

Kathleen smiled as she recalled some of the things that happened to her whilst she drove through the quiet North Devon lanes collecting her countryside rabbits. One day she was driving between Luscott towards Braunton when she rounded a bend to be met head on by a Polish airman riding his bike towards her at full pelt; she braked but he went up over her bonnet and landed in the hedge beside the van. Kathleen rushed out of the van to help the young man when she was mown down by a countryman to the first cyclist. She said they all landed in a heap in the hedge and fell about laughing!!

Kathleen and Alan Harris at Clovelly in 1940.

On another occasion she was driving from Bradiford up through Upcott towards Braunton when the van had a puncture. A group of prisoners of war was waiting for transport to take them to a nearby farm to work. They all set to work to change her wheel and she gave them a basket of plums.

Kathleen had married motor mechanic Alan Harris in 1937 and he'd joined the RAF for the duration of hostilities, and when he returned home in 1946 he joined his father Robert Harris and brother Robert in their building business R. Harris and Sons.

Robert Harris Snr was a stone mason who had worked on Saunton Court for the architect Sir Edwin Lutyens.

Alan's main responsibilities during these years were the concrete production for building private roads from the quarrying of stone at Little Silver Quarry, Bittadon, removing gravel from the Taw Estuary with the firm's two barges, the *Nellie* and *RH13*, and the production of concrete at their plant beside the River Taw at Barnstaple.

Many of the housing estates built in Braunton since 1950 have been the work of R. Harris and Sons or Harris and Reid, the company Alan set up with Alf Reid in the mid 1960s.

Alan's daughter Christine told me that her father had great pride in never building two houses exactly the same although she does remember him explaining to his father Robert Harris Snr the business acumen of building the large estate of houses being planned by Barnstaple Town Council to rehouse families affected by their Slum Clearance Programme of the mid 1950s.

Sailmakers

BRAUNDS OF SOUTH STREET – Christine Braund, who originally came from Fremington, is the widow of Richard (Dick) who worked for the family business of Braunds the Sailmakers in a workshop –loft – in South Street. The business is in the same place today.

As well as their workshop the Braunds also had a shop in Exeter Road, now part of Squires' Fish Resturant. This is where the business was carried on and the family lived in the four bedroom apartment above the shop.

Grandfather William Braund started the business and then his son Richard joined him and then his son Dick. William had two other sons – Tom, who worked as a sailmaker at Plymouth and Bert, who ran a taxi business in Braunton from his house right next to the railway crossing. This couldn't have been more useful for all those people who alighted from the trains at the station.

Dick had two sisters and when he was three his mother died of TB. Later his father remarried and had five more children. One of these, David, joined

The Sailmakers. Seated is William Alexander Braund the original owner of Braunds Sailmakers and tent makers. Behind are Dick Braund and his father Richard. This photograph was taken in the sailmakers loft in South Street where today Stephen and Paul Braund run Braund's Blinds.

the family firm and it is his sons Stephen and Paul who run a blind making business from the same workshop in South Street today. Dick didn't get on too well with his father and left the family business and went to work for Prideaux's Garage in Barnstaple, making soft top roofs for sports cars.

Later Dick, Christine and their five-week-old twin daughters moved back to Braunton and lived in one of the cottages that Dick's uncle had built from a farm he had bought in Chapel Street. Christine still lives in this cottage.

They went into making marquees for weddings and all kinds of events. When these were hired out they would transport the marquee to the venue and erect it and after the event return to dismantle it and take it back to their workshop. Once they were caught out when heavy snow fell when they were on Exmoor for a wedding reception. The men couldn't get home for several days but fortunately they found lodgings in some neighbouring cottages.

Tobbacconist and Confectioners – Atkins

Margaret Dent (née Atkins) was born in Braunton and lived above her parents' shop, Atkins the Confectioners and Tobacconists at the end of East Street on the Square; she remembers well the old Cross Tree outside their shop.

They had a maid called Ivy Tucker who lived in and as usual she was sent to collect the daily milk from Palmer's the Dairy in Heanton Street and on one occasion a half pound of butter. She was told to take Margaret with her. On the return journey Margaret wanted to carry the milk jug but Ivy said 'No' she could only carry the butter. Margaret says that in a fit of pique she remembers hurling it at a passing motor

Shoe Shop
Williams of South Street

Betsy Williams who was married to Richard, outside their shoe shop at 5, South Street.

Richard Williams standing – sitting are daughter May, his wife Betsy and son Bill. c.1903.

Atkins' Tobacconist's on the Square.

car and hitting it fair and square with splattered grease.

Undertakers – Clarke's

When Brian Clarke left school he worked in a bank at Combe Martin for nine years as well as acting as book-keeper for the family carpenter and undertakers business. One day the bank manager told him that when he came to work the next day to make sure he was spruced up and wearing his best suit and tie as one of the bosses was coming to inspect the branch.

Mr and Mrs Atkins.

In fact he was coming to see Brian at work as his manager had thought he was deserving of a better position higher up the banking tree. Soon after the visit Brian was offered a job in London in the Advanced Department. He turned it down because if he left it meant there wouldn't be anyone to do the firm's books and anyway he'd miss his hunting, shooting and fishing!

Brian left banking and joined his family in the undertaking business.

Brian's wife Jean also helped out with the business and one day when they were repatriating a body to London they had phoned ahead to say they would arrive between 1-1.15pm. When they arrived everyone had gone to lunch leaving a note to say they'd be back at 2pm. So Jean and Brian carried a 16 stone body in his coffin up a steep flight of stairs.

Another incident involving a heavy coffin was when they were driving along the M5 in the outside lane when one of their tyres burst. They pulled over to the hard shoulder and went to the rear of the vehicle only to realise they couldn't get to the spare wheel without moving the coffin! In full view of every passing car Jean could be seen holding up this large coffin while Brian struggled to remove the spare from underneath it! So remember, behind every scenario you witness in life there is a story – sometimes worth recording!

Wheelwright

Josiah James Huxtable who was a builder and carpenter and lived at Dean's Cottage.

Chapter 8

The Railway Station

The Age of Steam arrived in Braunton on 20 July, 1874. It was an event brought about by the people of Ilfracombe who for many years had petitioned for a railway line connecting their town to Barnstaple and then onwards on the mainline to Waterloo Station.

Ilfracombe had become a very popular holiday seaside town with paddle steamers arriving at the harbour and pier head every day with trippers and holidaymakers from along the coast as far as Bristol and across the Channel from Wales.

After the railway line opened the holiday business increased to such an extent that the single line had to be doubled. The work was completed in 1891. From the beginning of the twentieth century the London and South Western Railway along with the Great Western Railway operated the line and after nationalisation in 1948 it became the Western Region of British Rail.

At the height of its popularity between the World Wars there were as many as 24 passenger trains every day in both ways on the Ilfracombe to Barnstaple line and during the summer season some trains would be pulling as many as 10 coaches of holidaymakers heading for the resorts of Saunton, Croyde, Woolacombe and Ilfracombe and Combe Martin.

After leaving Barnstaple Town Station the line ran beside the estuary then just after Heanton Court it ran between Chivenor Airport (which during WWII became RAF Chivenor) and the main road until it stopped at Wrafton Station – an ages old name for the village behind.

During the war and up until the mid-1960s this was where all the airmen disembarked to return to camp after a visit to the hostelries of Barnstaple, or perhaps they were returning from further afield and home leave.

Through the Vellator gates and the next stop was Braunton Station, the largest on this line. It stood where Caen Street Car Park is today and where the goods sheds and station house have been found new

Braunton Railway Station.

uses. It was a busy station with a large staff to deal with the many passengers and a great deal of goods traffic.

The freight ranged from letters and parcels, as this was the way Royal Mail was moved around the country, to dairy produce being carried to towns and cities. Rabbits in their hundreds went every day to Smithfield Market in London and salmon caught in the estuary went to large London hotels.

Several coal merchants had depots close by, sand and gravel dredged from the estuary sometimes left for builders' yards further up the line, and it is without doubt that the railway had a depressing effect on the seafaring trade from Vellator. Flowers and vegetables from the Bulb Farm and the Great Field also made their way from this busy North Devon village to the wider world as did livestock such as horses, cattle and sheep.

In the early part of the twentieth century few private houses had telephones and communication was made by the telegraph system. It was from the railway station or the post office that telegrams were sent and received. It is interesting to see that in 1928 Braunton Station handled 704 telegrams and in 1936 this number had risen to 2312.

With four crossing gates everyone was made aware of the trains passing through the village. Every train stopped at the station which caused much frustration at the Caen Street crossing when a longer train stopped as it stretched across the road. This halted

Harry Evans who married cordwainer's daughter Eliza Reed. Harry was a signalman at Braunton Station in 1940s.

traffic along the busy Braunton to Saunton road, causing long tail-backs of frustrated drivers.

The earliest railway memories are from the early twentieth century and came from Dougie Reed whose great grandfather was a cordwainer (shoemaker) who lived at 17, Church Street with his wife Ellen and five children. One of their daughters, Eliza, was married to Harry Evans who was a railway signalman at Braunton Station. His great nephew Dougie remembers helping his Uncle Harry open the crossing gates by turning the huge cast iron wheel.

Nancy Barnes told us that in the 1920s her mother would catch the train on a Friday to Barnstaple to go to the Pannier Market before doing her shopping in the town. The cost of the return ticket was about 1/- which was the same price as the bus fare.

There were two types of train carriage – those with compartments with a corridor running down one side of the carriage and those with compartments and no corridor. Brian Williams like many of his contemporaries travelled to Barnstaple on the train every day to attend the Grammar School; Brian says there was many a game played along the corridors of the 'school' train and on one such occasion the game ended with several of the parents having the knock on their door from the Transport Police.

It all started as high spirits when a red cloth was produced and one boy took up the stance as the matador and another decided to be the bull. The

Minnie Lane from Broadgate Farm (fourth from the left) at Barnstaple Pannier Market.

R. L. Knight

game reached a raucous climax when the pretend cloak was whisked away and the 'bull' went straight through the glass in the door connecting the carriages! Result one boy with a very sore head and several more with tanned rear ends from infuriated fathers.

Others vividly recall the hundreds of holidaymakers who poured out of the trains on Saturdays after a long journey. Taxis and cars would be waiting to carry them to their destinations in the village or further afield to board and lodgings. Many families booked their holidays from one year to the next and still recall childhood days of beaches, cream teas and welcoming locals.

Vibrant memories of Braunton Railway Station come from Marilyn Abbott who has had a lifelong affinity with the station and steam trains. Her father worked at the station and they lived close by in Station Road. Her mother's association with the station also went back many years.

Marilyn's mother Betty Bamsey came to Braunton in 1931 when her mother died and moved in with the family of Jessie and Henry Hitchcock who lived at 11, Station Road. They ran the W.H. Smiths Newsagents kiosk – a round building that stood outside the station.

One of Betty's jobs was to help out with the early morning paper round before school each day. The newspapers were delivered to the station on the first train of the day. Later she also worked in the sweet kiosk at the Plaza Cinema until she was twenty-one when she was called up to join the ATS in 1942.

Betty often told her daughter Marilyn about the times when she was a young girl and with her friend Ruby Watts would fill their days with innocent fun and mischief. This often involved being the bane of the

Bill Mitchell playing in his garden with Betty Bamsey and his sister Vera.

Betty Bamsey when she was in the ATS during the war.

Station Master's life. Betty said Mr Stanley Liley was a very strict man but very much respected and he ran Braunton Station as if he was the captain of a ship. However, the girls would often tease him and play jokes on him. The two girls stayed friends all their lives and were forever to be found laughing at old memories of their childhood misdemeanours.

It is no wonder that Mr Liley told them it was the best day of his life when he saw both girls on opposite platforms as they went their separate ways during wartime service. Ruby went to Ilfracombe and Betty to Honiton.

Marilyn's father Ken Abbott came from a family of railway workers and he joined the railway when he was fifteen as the lowest grade porter. He worked at every station between Exeter and Ilfracombe.

It was 1940 and Ken was sent to Braunton to cover for someone who had been called up for war service. Station Master Liley had arranged that Ken would lodge with the Hitchcock family at 11, Station Road, which is where he met Betty, his future wife.

In conversation with his son Ken, he told him that there were seven staff on the station when he arrived, the Station Master who was the kingpin, two signalmen, two porters and a clerk and then Ken as the newly appointed junior porter.

Caen Street from the railway crossing.

Ruby Watts.

The station was always busy, said Ken, but what would you expect as Braunton was then the biggest village in England. Every day there was plenty of freight moving around from the flower farm, the pottery and the basket factory to name but a few.

In 1941 when he was twenty-one Ken joined the RAF and he told Marilyn that he felt he'd had good grounding for the services as the railway was very strict on discipline and he even found the RAF easier. He served not only in this country but also in North Africa, Italy and Sicily. At the end of the war he returned to Chivenor and was demobbed and then retrained as a railway signalman.

The hard winter of 1947 saw him working in the signal box at Mortehoe Station where he was snowed in overnight and unable to get home after his shift. This made it difficult for Betty who was expecting a baby and worrying when Ken would get home. Unlike today, there was no telephone communication between Ken's work and home.

From 1950 Ken became permanent signalman at Wrafton and Marilyn remembers Sunday afternoons in the summer when her father was on late turn and her mother and sister Alison would pack up a picnic and take it down to the signal-box to have tea with

him. Sometimes he would allow them to play at turning the wheel and pulling the levers.

Marilyn also remembers another visit to the signal box and that was on the day she passed the 11+ exam. The children at Caen Street School who had passed the exam and lived in the village were told they could go home and tell their parents. Marilyn lived the closest but was the last pupil back to the classroom which caused much comment. She didn't tell anyone there was no-one at home, so she cycled to Wrafton to excitedly impart her good news to her father.

Even as a teenager Marilyn was fascinated by steam trains and knew many of the drivers and firemen who worked on this line and sometimes she was allowed to ride on the footplate. One day when on Wrafton Station her father arranged for her to ride on the footplate to Ilfracombe. The engine was turned around on the turntable at Ilfracombe for the journey back to Braunton. Once there the driver pulled up opposite her home at Station Road and allowed Marilyn to blow the engine's whistle before jumping down onto the track, hurrying through the hedge, across the road and into her home where she proudly announced to her mother that it was she who had just blown the whistle. Her mother wasn't too pleased as the noise had woken her young brother Ken from his slumbers.

In 1966 the Wrafton signal box closed and Ken along with Fred Woodley became Station Foremen, working alternate shifts.

Ken was on duty when the last train went through Braunton on the evening of Saturday 3 October, 1970. Earlier in the day the train had been full of people wanting to ride on it for the last time. Marilyn had taken this train both into Barnstaple and on its return

Bulbs from the Bulb Farm being loaded onto D828 'Magnificent' in 1965.

Ken Abbott outside the Wrafton signal box.

Marilyn Abbott and her brother Ken.

memento of the occasion. She still treasurers it today.

Marilyn explained to me that although these closures were a great inconvenience to many rail customers they caused a tremendous upheaval to the railwaymen and their families. She explained that her father finished work at Braunton Station that Saturday evening and the next day he had to leave his home and family and move to Bristol. He started work as the supervisor in the Red Star parcel office at Bristol Templemeads Station. The family lived a disjointed life with Ken away until they found a home to move into. Marilyn remained in Braunton. On his retirement in 1986 Ken and Betty moved to Exmouth.

Today the railway line from Barnstaple to Braunton is just as popular as ever but as the Tarka Trail – a walking and cycle path that gives a great deal of pleasure to both local people and visitors.

journey and said she had felt so sad to be there at the end of an era. However, she still remembers with pride, when she alighted from the train at Braunton her father gave her his station master's cap as a

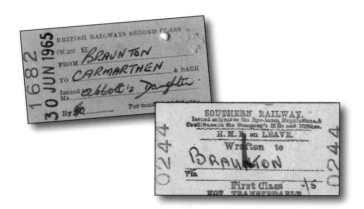

A GWR train passes Heanton Court as an Atlantic Coast Air Service plane takes off from Chivenor Aerodrome.

R. L. Knight

Chapter 9
Memories of WWII

Many villages in our countryside were hardly aware that the world was at war during 1939 to 1945, but this couldn't be said of Braunton. We were situated on the edge of the Atlantic Ocean where our shipping was in constant danger from enemy submarines and aircraft.

In 1940 what had been Chivenor Farms was bought by the government and Royal Air Force Chivenor flew into action as a Coastal Command base. There were several air accidents during the war as Heanton churchyard bears witness and some enemy aircraft came to grief whilst trying to make it home to Germany.

The most bizarre of stories is when a German JU88 bomber landed on the runway at Chivenor and its crew realised they had landed on enemy territory rather than the French airstrip they had planned. They had been fooled by a decoy radio beacon set up by the British to mimic a German one. The crew were sent to an internment camp but not before being marched along Exeter Road and Caen Street to the railway station.

When war was declared Braunton along with the rest of the country dealt with the shock and then in great British style got on with the job! Shelters were built, blackout curtains made, gas masks distributed and ration books organised. And Dr. Ritchie was put in charge of the Invasion Committee.

The Invasion Committee Book is kept at the Braunton Museum and lists the action plans for such things as billeting, citizens advice, doctors and nursing (trained and St John Ambulance), Fire Guards, Home Guard, wardens and police. There is also information on what they had at their disposal such as 14 tractors, 37 horses and carts and Mr Dennis of Knowle promised 100 picks and shovels at a moment's notice. Housewives were listed in order of streets and their responsibilities, like who would

The Home Guard meeting in the Assembly Hall at the Senior School.

provide hot drinks, washing facilities and who could deal with gas splashed victims and who could be 'generally useful'!

Mr Scoins was the food officer, Mr Prior of the London Inn was in charge of the Fire Guards, Reg Slee was responsible for the emergency water supply and Reg Isaac was responsible for the mortuaries (of which there were three). Mr Hancock of the Dairy, East Street was the sewer contractor, Mr Babb was in charge of the rest centre at the Senior School and Sgt Litten had six regular police officers and 30 special constables under his command. They had information regarding water supply, where food and medical stocks would be kept and how they would evacuate RAF Chivenor in the event that Braunton was invaded by the enemy.

Memories of life in Braunton during WWII are mostly not of fear, hardship and deprivation but of hard work, making do and making fun – especially when the American Army arrived!

The Americans set up camp along the Saunton Road. They built roads throughout Braunton Burrows and fenced off Saunton beach from public use. They used these areas as training grounds as well as Barnstaple/Bideford Bay and the estuary for amphibious vehicles. All in preparation for the D-

Jack and Gwenllan Woolway.

Jack Woolway, daughter Nancy in the WRAF, Mrs Woolway, daughter Eirlys in WRAF and son Dick Woolway who was in the REME.

Sisters – Poppy, Nancy, Edith and Eirlys.

Day Invasion. There were military police at entrance and exit roads to the village and even on the trains when the soldiers went into Barnstaple for R and R (rest and relaxation).

Some people were not happy at the arrival of our American cousins – usually fathers of daughters! But the children of the village were quickly won over and the people of Braunton soon showed our imposed guests some good old British hospitality.

Margaret Beatrice Poppy Woolway has always been known as Poppy as she was born on Armistice Day 1930. Her parents were great supporters of the British Legion as have Poppy and her husband John been for over 50 years.

Poppy's father Jack was a builder and carpenter. With his Welsh wife and five children he settled in Mill Style, where Poppy was born.

Jack had fought in France in WWI with the Devonshire Regiment and when WWII started he re-enlisted with the Devons. He survived a harrowing time at Dunkirk but would never discuss with his family its horrors. He spent the remainder of his war in Exeter where he trained the Home Guard units from around the South West region.

Back in Braunton Poppy's mother Gwen had RAF servicemen billeted on them. To this day Poppy can hear her mother recite their names as she tried to come up with the one she wanted – 'Eddie, Teddy, Neddie, Freddie!'

There was a forces canteen in East Street where the servicemen could have meals. Poppy says she liked the Americans as they always had plenty of sweets and chocolates which they shared with her. After the war the parents of one of the G.I.s sent the Woolway family a box of biscuits and chocolates as a thank-you for the kindness shown to their son.

Poppy was nine when WWII broke out and she was at Caen Street School. She later moved to the senior school and left at fourteen. She used to work at the Bulb Farm and remembers it was back breaking work but says it earned a few pennies.

Two boys who were evacuated from Plymouth lived near Brian Clarke at Down Lane. One day they all went out for a picnic near the White House. The two evacuees got into difficulty in the water and the eldest boy – Clary Mills – nearly drowned. He was saved by a human chain grabbing him and passing him along until he was out of danger. Bert Braund who was with them went in his taxi to fetch Dr Ritchie.

A Beaufort plane crashed at the top of Down Lane in 1941. Brian heard it from his house and when he arrived at the scene the firemen were already there. The plane's engine had rolled down over two fields and ended up at the back door of Mr Buckingham's house.

A Super Fortress crashed near Kennel Cottages on Park Road. Bert French, who was home on leave, managed to pull the two crew to safety out of the plane. The next day the Headmaster Leonard Ash lined up all the boys and told them that they had to take everything back to the plane that they may have removed from it. Brian thought it would be a wise move to return the dinghy paddle he had taken.

Brian Ellis also recalls how during the war the farmers would come to the school to get volunteers to help in the fields while their farm workers were away in the armed forces.

Brian used to deliver meat to Chivenor on his butcher's bike. The basket on the front was massive and it was hard work peddling. Later he was allowed to drive the van or a car with a trailer and there was so much meat in the trailer the car couldn't pull away. Several people had to put their weight behind the car to move it from the shop. When he arrived at the camp he knew that if he stopped he'd never pull away again so when he was driving towards the barrier he'd gesticulate to the sentry. The barrier would go up and Brian would sail through with as much speed as he could muster.

After the war Brian's father Harry and Barnstaple butcher Percy Brend bought the forest of nissen huts the American soldiers had lived in whilst stationed in the fields along Saunton Road. The huts were sold to many a farmer who bought them to give their pigs a good home!

For farmer Roland Dibble wartime holds many memories especially of the Yankees. One day he was working in a field (the one next to the football field today) when a massive bulldozer burst through the hedge in front of him. Shocked and stunned, Roland asked the driver what he thought he was up to, only to be told that all the fields from there into Braunton had been requisitioned and he would have to leave!

Roland has memories of the mess the American soldiers made of the road whilst this camp was being built. He said the mud was so deep on the road they couldn't ride their bikes through it and when walking to the village they had to cover their shoes and trousers with sacking.

Roland also recalls the Bulb Farm opposite his farm where fields were turned into tank parks – row after row of them. This was all a build up for the D-Day landings and Roland recalls that just as the U.S. troops appeared out of the blue, they also suddenly disappeared.

John Avery who was five when war broke out and lived with his parents at Cross Farm, tells a similar story when he says the Americans based on the Saunton Road camp had complete authority on the south side of the A361. If they wanted a field they would just take it over without asking or informing the farmer. John remembers that when they were bringing stone from the quarries to make the roads through their camp they would leave mud and debris ankle deep through the village.

Wartime rules were that every household had to billet servicemen or evacuees if possible. His parents took in a succession of personnel from RAF Chivenor. John says it was party time every night. The servicemen and their wives who came to live with them would play darts and cards after their evening meal. The table was laden with food and life seemed to be good to his young eyes. But of course it wasn't as sometimes airmen went on a mission and didn't come back. He remembers one pilot that was shot down and another who was killed trying to escape from Stalag Luft 3.

Brian Williams remembers all the children at school being issued with gas masks and having to practice what to do when the air raid warning sounded. He said a large shelter was built at the Caen Street gateway of the school playground, and the children didn't always wait for the air raid warning as they became used to the sound of enemy aircraft overhead when German bombers headed for the Welsh coast. On the way back they would drop any remaining bombs they were carrying on Chivenor. Not always being accurate in their aim, Braunton was left vulnerable.

Brian lived with his parents on the Square and when they were at home at these times the family would run for cover to the larder under the stairs at the back of their men's outfitters shop.

Brian told me of the American soldiers who used to be on guard duty at Town End and how he got on friendly terms with some of them especially as they had sweets, cigarettes and chewing gum – items which were strictly rationed to British people.

One evening Brian was in conversation with one of these guards who was showing off the use of his knife. He said he could slit down the back of Brian's jacket without him knowing it. And to prove his point he did just that! Brian said his father may have been a tailor with the wherewithal to repair the damaged coat, but when he got home that evening 'hell hath no fury' like a father whose son had had his jacket slit from collar to waist for a bet.

Brian also remembers the dances at the Parish Hall and going to watch the Americans jiving and jitterbugging and their equal expertise with wooing the local young ladies.

When Brian tried a little of this wooing himself after the VE Day celebrations with a girl who was on holiday from London, this fifteen year old young man was whisked home by his father and given the third degree as to where he had been and what he had been up to!

Norman Venner, who lived with his aunt and uncle at Kupke's Bakery, recalls when the American soldiers marched into the village and seeing one of them chewing gum he shouted out to him, ' Got any gum chum?' The soldier threw some to him and Norman put it straight into his mouth ready to enjoy some illicit pleasure BUT Aunt Winifred came along and soon relieved him of his ill-gotten gift. Norman doesn't know if it was his aunt's dislike of gum or of the Americans!

Atkins Confectioners and Tobacconists on the Square at the end of East Street saw plenty of our wartime guests from across The Pond. Daughter of the owners Margaret Dent told me that during the war her mother's younger sister Pat lived with them and Margaret was envious that Pat went to the village dances but Margaret's father said she was too young. However, she was allowed to sit up in the balcony to watch the American and British servicemen dancing with the local girls. She especially loved to watch them doing the jitterbug, palais glide, foxtrot and barn dances.

She may not have been allowed to go to the dances but she was permitted to go to the classes held in the hall. And I don't know if her father knew, but Margaret said the servicemen went to them as well!

Some of the shops in the village would close at 6pm and re-open at 10pm for a couple of hours, no doubt to make the most of the custom from servicemen returning from Barnstaple or leaving the local public houses.

Elaine Christie was five when her family moved to Braunton in 1942. Her father was in the RAF and was posted to Chivenor. She especially remembers the Americans soldiers when they dug up the cricket pitch to lay a pipe line (probably a pipe from their tented camp to the sewage works at Vellator). And the 'Yanks' who came to call hoping to persuade her mother and her friend to go dancing with them at the Parish Hall. Elaine's mother asked one of them when he last wrote to his mother and when he answered that he couldn't remember she asked for his mother's address and she wrote telling her that he was OK. The two women corresponded for many years and in 1947 Elaine and her two sisters received a large parcel containing three dolls. Elaine still has her doll sixty-seven years later.

Going back to Clarke's Dairy and Café in Exeter Road – John Clarke continues his story that when the war came to an end the café side of the business,

Elaine Christie's doll sent to her from an American soldier's mother.

which had been a great success during those years, also dwindled. His father Reg returned to run the dairy and his Uncle Fred returned to his duties on Braunton Station. In fact John recalls that the family had quite a good set-up going. Fred would be on the station and when the holidaymakers alighted from the train and those who had not made any prior booking for accommodation, Fred would call up Bob Ridge and his taxis and send the travellers off to either his home where Phyllis did B&B or John's mother's house in Barton Lane where she also catered for those needing a bed and breakfast. In this way the wheels of commerce kept turning and the visitors got some Devonshire homely comforts.

Cousins Vera and Dot Mitchell in their Land Army uniforms.

Dorothy Mitchell, who was working as a house-maid at Heanton Court in 1939, was called up to do war work and out of the shortlist she was given she chose Shapland and Petter's factory in Barnstaple which was making general munitions. Dot made haversacks – called 'flats' – for soldiers and white coats for doctors.

After working at Shaplands for two years the younger women had to leave to work in the NAAFI or the Women's Land Army. Dot joined the Land

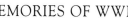

Lunch time for the workers at the Bulb Farm.

Land Army girls at the Bulb Farm L-R: Pat Pethick, Katie Newman, Dot Mitchell. Kneeling Marjorie ? and Beat Featherstone.

Getting a lift on the trailer.

A happy band of Land Army girls.

Land Army girls dressed in their uniforms for the wedding of one of the group. Left to right: *Eileen ?, Sylvia ?, Marjorie ?, unknown, Vera Mitchell, Blanche ?, Beatrice Milligan, Pat Brown, Dorothy Mitchell, Marjorie ?, unknown, Pam Richards, unknown, Betty ? and Nelly Sweet.*

Army and enjoyed every minute of it although when she described some of the conditions they worked under I think that probably the sunshine days drowned out the harsh memories.

Dot and her cousin Vera Mitchell stayed together through the war and have many shared memories of working at the Bulb Farm in Sandy Lane.

She recalled that before the war Mrs Snell would grow daffodils, iris and tulips and the fields would be ablaze with spring colours. A fond memory was of going up to the Beacon during a royal celebration and looking down on the fields in strips of red white and blue flowers. But during wartime the flower growing had to be put on hold and the ground was used to grow potatoes, beetroot, cauliflowers, Brussels sprouts, tomatoes and sunflowers.

There were 10 large glass houses of tomatoes and during the summer this was really hot work. Dot remembers that opposite was a field where the American soldiers were camped and they would send over fruit juice and polony sausage for the girls.

An equally vibrant memory was how gruelling it was to work in the fields in the winter and how her hands were red raw with the cold when they had to break the ice on the water troughs to clean Brussel sprouts before packing them.

She also remembers what a hard task-master Mrs Snell was – there was no slacking by anyone and if they took too long in the toilets they were reprimanded. No one was allowed to smoke and even when the women were wet through by the heavy rain

they were not permitted to change their clothes until the end of their shift.

All this aside, Dot has fond memories of those war years and the women she shared her life with and has kept in touch with them since.

Dot met her husband Donald Davies on a blind date when her best friend Pat persuaded her to go along to make up a foursome. Donald was in the RAF at Chivenor but only for a few months before he was posted to Gibraltar for much of the war. They married at St Brannock's church in 1944 and when Donald left the RAF in 1945 they lived in Donald's home in South Wales before returning to her home in Braunton where she lives today.

When Joan Incledon was in service at Saunton with the Lycett household it was 1940 and the beach was

One of the reunions of the wartime friends.

78

Dorothy Mitchell marries Donald Davies at St Brannock's church in 1944.

out of bounds as the servicemen were practising with live ammunition and aircraft were using the bay as a bombing range.

She remembers the time at the house when a mine was washed up on the beach and they were all made to move to the bedrooms at the back of the house in case it exploded.

In 1944 when Joan was eighteen she decided to do her war work at Chivenor in the carpenters' shop repairing airplanes. Dick Atkins, a skilled carpenter, was also employed there, and Joan remembers how kind he was to the unskilled women who didn't know what to do. She said that at first they had to put up with a lot of leg pulling but eventually when the men could see that the girls could be useful they all worked well together

Later Joan worked at the Bulb Farm and loved it as she appreciated being out in the fresh air which was much healthier than working in an enclosed space with oil heaters and airplane glue.

A little known fact is that 62, South Street was for a while used as a kibbutz. In February 1940 a group of 36 Jewish refugee teenagers lived in the three storey house. They came from all over Europe and from diverse backgrounds which caused tensions in the household.

The idea was to teach them agriculture by working at the Bulb Farm and to accustom them to the kibbutz lifestyle. Most of the girls carried out household duties although some worked with the men at the farm and some of the men worked on local farms.

This group of youngsters were an off-shoot of another commune at Bydown House, Swimbridge, and from the start the project seems to have been poorly funded. The house was ill equipped for so many people. In the first week they only had 22 blankets for 36 people and they had to share five towels!

Supplies and equipment eventually arrived but the group was faced with more problems. The main one was the harshness of the long hours worked at the Bulb Farm. Bending and picking flowers for ten hours a day with only half an hour for lunch and tea-break was considered too much physical strain for the youngsters, with 10/- a week pay instead of the £2 adults got.

Added to the day work was the half an hour it took to walk to and from the farm. No wonder the organiser complained that the young people were too exhausted to study English in the evenings, let alone wash or eat their supper.

When they had to start work at 6.15am which meant leaving South Street at 5.30am in the morning this was probably the straw that broke the camel's back. One of the group sought help from a member of the Refugee Committee, Mrs Greaves, who ran a chemist's shop in Barnstaple. She in turn called upon Maurice Prince who ran the Regal Cinema in Barnstaple and was related to members of the parent organisation in London.

A letter was sent to the Bulb Farm giving notice for the teenager's departure and they returned to Bydown House.

This story can be found in full in Helen Fry's book *Jews in North Devon During the Second World War.*

Helen Fry's father-in-law David Fry from Knowle tells me that he was used to seeing servicemen – English and American Army and RAF – everywhere towards the end of the war. There were frequent convoys of service vehicles passing through the village between Braunton, Woolacombe and Westward Ho! And when he was at Knowle David would fill up water bottles in return for chewing gum.

It was one of these convoys that knocked John Clarke to the ground when he was trying to cross Exeter Road near his grandfather's dairy. John was carried back to the shop and he says he's sure he played on his injuries for longer than necessary as the American soldiers kept visiting him with gifts of sweets, cookies and gum.

As children of Caen Street School they were taken by army lorry to the American camp on the Saunton Road for Christmas parties. On 5 June, 1944 the school children walked from their classrooms to St Brannock's churchyard to witness a tree being planted to honour the American servicemen who had worked to restore the churchyard after years of neglect.

Annie Fry behind the counter of the Knowle shop and Post Office.

David notes several interesting people lived at Church Hill, Knowle during wartime. The most mysterious was Mrs Myler, a recluse who lived in a house among the trees. It was David's job to deliver her groceries from his mother's shop and he had strict instructions never to knock or call out to her but to leave her shopping inside the back door. On one of these occasions David saw a revolver on a table. This along with radio aerials fixed high up in the trees confirmed to David that Mrs Myler was a spy!

He later discovered that in fact Mrs Myler, who spoke fluent German, was working for the war department listening in to enemy radio messages. On one occasion she intercepted signals from a German submarine just off of Lundy Island and the Navy depth charged it and arrested the crew when it surfaced.

David said his mother and father, who ran the post office at Knowle, must have been privy to many wartime secrets as all Mrs Myler's telegrams went through their hands.

A well-known character of this time – and for some years later – was George 'Gandy' Clarke who lived with his parents Thomas and Lillian at the bottom of Church Hill. George has been described as a dare-devil who was a spitfire pilot during the war. He would sometimes fly his plane very low, upside down with his canopy open, over his mother's house whilst waving to her.

George (Gandy) Clarke with John Clarke on his knee.

George was shot down twice over France but escaped and returned to England. Having survived the war he started a garage business in Braunton. He didn't give up on his love of speed and would be the bane of the local policemen who would always have him on their radar. He survived several serious car crashes.

When Mrs Myler died in 1948 David Fry's father Edmund, George Clarke and Alfie Mock were three of the coffin bearers at the Ilfracombe church. After the service George drove the other two men back to Knowle in his usual frenetic manner. Suddenly he swerved off the main road and up Church Hill and as they hit a bump in the road the two gentlemen sitting in the back seat in their morning suits and bowler hats hit the roof of the car, pushing the hats firmly down over their ears!! David says his father never travelled with George Clarke again.

Another Church Hill resident was Mrs McCulloch, the mother of BBC broadcaster 'Uncle Mac' who used to have a programme, 'Children's Hour', every weekday afternoon. Still remembered with great affection are the warm dulcet tones of Uncle Mac saying," Hello children everywhere". Uncle Mac or Derek McCulloch wrote several children's books and one day his mother gave David one of them with an inscription inside.

Today Saunton Sands Hotel with its brilliant white coat stands out on the headland over the beach, but in the war the last thing the War Department wanted was a beacon that would inform enemy ships and aircraft just where they were, so the hotel was hidden from view with camouflage paint.

No longer was it an hotel but a school. In 1940 the Duke of York's Royal Military School was evacuated from Dover after the school took a direct hit by rockets fired from the French coast.

Some of the pupils (known affectionately as Dukie's) had been sent to the Queen Victoria School in Dunblane, Scotland which left Saunton Sands Hotel accommodating 360 boys.

Barnstaple and Ilfracombe were out of bounds to the boys and they didn't venture into Braunton or Saunton very often but David Fry remembers them attending the Plaza Cinema in Exeter Road as they usually seized his school cap and threw it onto the stage!

Locally the boys were known for their band which performed for different fund raising events and they led the Victory Parade.

Art Cockerill says in an e-mail that he has fond memories of North Devon as a member of the school band, playing in Barnstaple and Exeter and they presented Barnstaple's Mayoral office with two of their silver bugles. He also had some not-so-fond memories of 'picking spuds' for local farmers in cold, wet and soggy weather. Many of the boys worked at the Bulb Farm on Saturdays to earn themselves some pocket money.

Pupils from the Duke of York's Royal Military School at the back of their school which was the Saunton Sands Hotel during WWII.

Gladys Raby who lived in Heanton Street as a child, worked at Saunton Sands Hotel when it was taken over by the Duke of York's School. She said the school was run on military lines with the boys in houses named after military commanders – Wellington, Marlborough, Woolf, Clive and others. Each unit had its own Regimental Sergeant Major and Matron and discipline was very strict.

Twice mayor of Barnstaple and head teacher Ian Scott is an ex- 'Dukie' although not old enough to have been at Saunton. However, he has met up with several men who were there, one being Warrant Officer Taylor who told Ian of his appointment as a teacher. It was his first night at Saunton and he found the boys unusually cheeky or sleepy. Investigation revealed the latest entrants of young boys had just arrived and as some of them were small enough to fit through the bars of the wine cellar window they had, under orders of their elders acted as couriers with the bottles of wine!

The school returned to Dover in the spring of 1946 and Saunton Sands Hotel grew to be the landmark of excellence it is today.

Vera (Micky) Coats – Wren.

The Dukies marching back to their school from Croyde.

*On the left is Olna Welch of Buckland Barton in the
Air Ambulance Service.*

*L/Cpl Ernest Jenkins
of the Devonshire Reg.*

*Christopher Irwin, Bomber
Command – lost in a bombing raid
over Germany in 1942.*

Dorothy Butler (third from left, middle row) – WRAAF 1940.

Wartime Weddings

Micky and Ernest Jenkins

Ken and Eileen Salter who had both served in the Navy during the war married at St Brannock's church in 1945. Ken later joined the Devon Constabulary.

VE Day Celebrations

South Street celebrates.

Chapter 10

The Thin Blue Line

The Long Arm of the Law in Braunton relied on one sergeant and one constable in the early 1900s. The police station was in the row of houses in Heanton Street – at the time the main road into the village from Barnstaple.

Church Street blacksmith's daughter Margaret Elliott used to watch out of her bedroom window that overlooked St Brannock's churchyard as the constable brought any drunken rowdy to the lock-up in the churchyard. She would see the constable manhandle his prisoner into the stone-built shed, lock the door and leave him to sober up. Margaret recalls how the prisoner would barrack the world for his misfortune long into the night.

With the Exeter Road being opened in 1931 the newly-built police station on the corner of Barton Lane and Exeter Road stood at the gateway of the village. Several of the men and women in this chapter lived in the accommodation provided by the station over the years.

In 1910 Arthur Edward John Chapple (known as Art) was born the fifth of the six children of John and Grace Chapple of Lower Winsham, Knowle He was their only son and two years old when his

PC 10 Arthur Edward John Chapple – known as Art.

father died of pneumonia. With his mother and three older sisters they moved into Chapel Cottage.

After schooling at Caen Street Board School Art went to work at Dennis's sawmills as a carpenter. His mother died when he was twenty and four years later he left Chapel Cottage to join the Devonshire Constabulary.

After he married Evelyn Lovering – who had been the companion to Mrs Snell of the Bulb Farm – they had their son Ronald in 1942 at Ashburton and their daughter Christine in 1947 at Cheriton Fitzpane. Two years later the family returned to North Devon for good when Art was posted to Barnstaple and in 1958 his final move was a return to his roots in Braunton where the family took up residence in the Exeter Road Police Station.

It is said that Art Chapple could turn his hand to most things and was most meticulous in their execution and he had an honest no-nonsense approach to life.

Totnes born Don Hill joined the Devon Constabulary in 1951. He arrived at Braunton after probationary training at Sidmouth, and also posted to Braunton was police constable John Greenwood. They each had a bedroom on the first floor

Arthur Chapple's family in Knowle in 1929. Back row L-R: eldest sister Annie, Florence, brother-in-law Joseph Adams, sister Elsie and Jane. Front row: Edmund Fry Annie's husband (they lived at the Stores and Post Office in Knowle), mother Grace Chapple and Arthur. Father John Chapple died when Arthur was only two years old.

Motor Patrol Constable Art Chapple driving Lord Fortescue on an official visit.

Braunton Police Station and police houses on Exeter Road.

above the charge room at the police station.

There were no cooking facilities so the single men had to take all their meals away from the station. Breakfast, dinner, tea and supper were provided by Mrs Welch at Vellator Terrace, South Street. This meant a walk down Barton Lane and back again for every meal.

Between the hours of 10pm and 6am the police station was not manned, and any incoming phone calls or callers to the station had to be dealt with by Don or his colleague. So in fact they were never off duty!

During the three years that Don was at Braunton he had two sergeants, Craddock and Les Davy, five beat constables and three motor patrol constables. These had the use of a shiny black Wolseley car and if necessary the sergeant's own car could be pressed into service, for which he could claim a mileage allowance. As for the beat constables, there was only one station bicycle, but they were told they could use their own cycles and claim a wear and tear allowance! They also had a boot allowance of 10/- (50p) a quarter.

Don recalled that when he first joined the police force at Sidmouth there was only one typewriter in the station which was for the exclusive use of the station sergeant. The constables were advised to buy their own and claim £2 a quarter typewriter allowance for which they could get free ribbons and correcting fluid!

Two outstanding memories Don has of his 1952 to 1955 service at Braunton. The first will always be the most spectacular of his police service and that is when between 50 and 60 policemen of the Devon Constabulary were selected for duty in London at the Coronation on 2 June 1953. All police forces were living in tents in St James' Park and Don with the rest of the Devon Constabulary lined the route along Birdcage Walk. He remembers vividly seeing the Queen and Duke of Edinburgh in the Golden Coach.

When the procession returned to Buckingham Palace they stood on guard along the Mall. He said he can still picture the magnificent colours, the mili-

tary precision and the larger than life Queen of Tonga who was a lovely smiling lady who waved to everyone.

The other incident will remain as the most devastating of Don's career. It was after a great storm in the winter of 1954 when a ship went down off the coast of Southern Ireland with the loss of all hands. Don said he took a phone-call from a lady dog walker who had found a body on Saunton beach. And along with his sergeant and another colleague he hurried to the scene and later they were joined by more policemen, firemen and St John Ambulance personnel. In all eight bodies of drowned seamen were found on the beach and many others were washed up along the North Devon Coast. Don recalls the enormity of having to deal with so many lost in such tragic circumstances.

On a lighter note Don told me that one day whilst on duty in Caen Street he heard a friendly female voice call out to him, "Don Hill what are you doing here?" The young lady was a friend of Don's family back home in Totnes who didn't know that Don had moved to Braunton. She was now living in the area and invited him to join the Young Conservatives. Don had to get permission from his sergeant and was only allowed to take part in the social events. It was at one of these occasions that he met his future wife Joan Gear.

Joan's father Charles Gear was a piano tuner and organ repairer and was in partnership with Gilbert Welch (where Don had his daily meals). These two men had a shop in the Square (today Marston's Holiday Cottages) and they also sold musical instruments, sheet music, records, gramophones and record players.

Don reminisced about the life of a village bobby in the 1950s/'60s. His beat covered many parishes from Shirwell to Marwood, Bittadon, Arlington, Loxhore and Kentisbury and between 1955 and 1961 his only transport was a bicycle! Although they had a telephone in the police house there was no other form of communication once he left his home. When he was away from the police house his wife had to take over the job of general factotum by answering phone calls and dealing with anyone who came to the police office. As Don pointed out the country policeman's job was really a two man job – so it was pay one get one free!

One day when Don had cycled to Kentisbury on the A39 a message came through that a car accident had happened on the dangerous bends near Arlington. When he arrived at the scene he found the car upside down and one person sitting on a wall. Don was concerned that there were other people trapped in the upturned vehicle. However, those fears were soon put to one side when the man on the wall drew a gun and threaten him with it!

The incident became intense for a while but Don

could see that this young man was very shocked from the accident and he was able finally to relieve him of his firearm which on closer inspection was found to be a starting pistol. The man had just held up a post office at Barbrook and in a bid to get away as far and as fast as possible had taken the bends too fast. Don was awarded a Chief Constable's Commendation for his handling of this event.

In 1961 Don was issued with a Triumph 350cc motorcycle with a police radio. Now he was the man with faster wheels and he was called upon to go to Lynton and Lynmouth to help control the heavy holiday traffic in the summer months.

Sgt Owen John Thomas Osborn – known to all as Ossie Osborn.

Another of Don's jobs as a 'Country Copper' was to attend farms when it was time for the sheep to be dipped in chemicals which killed off flies and their maggots. Other times Don visited farms to make sure that the hedgerows alongside the roads were kept in good trim and there was no mud or manure left on the highway and that fences and hedges were fit for purpose when it came to keeping stock away from the road. Anyone who has driven around a country road and come face to face with a big, fat, healthy cow or a flock of sheep knows only too well how much we appreciated the policeman who made sure the farms on his patch were well fenced and animal proof.

Another of Don's briefs was to attend Barnstaple Cattle Market on a Tuesday and Friday where he had his own office (for all those forms to be issued and signed!). As swine fever was such a threat in those times all pigs and piglets had to be monitored through the market. And once sold they couldn't be resold for twenty-eight days. In order to eliminate animal diseases all cattle transport had to be thoroughly hosed down between visiting one farm and another. Don had to make sure this took place at the cattle market.

In 1965 Don and Joan and their family moved to another country station at Witheridge and after five years he was posted back to Braunton where he remained for the rest of his service. The last five years of that was as Coroner's Officer.

Since his retirement from the Devon and Cornwall Constabulary in 1981 Don worked with Trading Standards specializing in everything to do with the regulations of diseases in animals – back to his roots in the job he knew so much about as a country bobby. Now in his second retirement this nonagenarian is an active member of several aspects of Braunton life.

Born in April 1918 Cornishman Owen John Thomas

Osborn – famously known to all as Ossie – joined the Devon Constabulary because the height restriction for the Cornwall Force was 6ft tall and Ossie was only 5ft. 11ins!

He served in several parts of Devon, mainly in the CID, but completed his service at Braunton between 1963 and 1969. Ossie, moved with his family into the police house adjoining the station.

From the start he regarded Braunton as if it belonged to him and any wrongdoing he took as a personal insult. Before long the local criminals took their activities to pastures new!

Ossie's daughter Barbara Dadds gave me her thoughts about her father and his impact on the welfare of the people of Braunton.

"As a policeman everyone was in awe of him. He was a big man, both in stature and personality. He had a presence that is difficult to define, but when he walked into a room everyone was aware he was there. Local people felt safe in their beds and still talk about him to this day with a great deal of affection.

"There are many incidents during his time at Braunton that should be told. Dad was a police officer during the time that a clip around the ear was acceptable (even expected) and there's many a local who was in receipt of such a reprimand. Dad would then take them home to their parents, who would give them another, as they appreciated the fact that their children were not up in front of the courts!

"In the mid 1960s a local Barnstaple lad was causing a lot of trouble at one of the dances in the Parish Hall. In those days there were often problems between Barnstaple and Braunton youths – who were the toughest, who attracted most women and so on. On this particular evening, Dad was called to sort out the trouble. One of the lads gave him a load of lip and said something to the effect that if Dad thought he was a hard man he'd show him what a hard man was really like. He then proceeded to lay into my father, who hit the lad so hard that he spun around the walls of the Parish Hall!

"Then there was the time Dad was notified of a burglary in progress at the jewellery shop in the village. It was snowing at the time and Dad followed the footprints from the shop to where a car had been parked and along the tracks to a farm at West Down. He knocked at the door, which was answered by a male. When he was told he was being arrested for burglary the lad asked what had led Dad to his address. And the surprised man confessed to the crime!

"On the other hand, Dad was gentle giant and to see him cradle a baby or talk to a young child showed a completely different side of him. I particularly remember the day he recovered the body of a small child from the river and will never forget his face when he came home that evening; it was obvious that he had been sobbing.

"One day he decided to keep chickens in the garden of the police station. My brother and I gave them names and eventually they started to lay eggs. Then came the time when they were ready for the kitchen table! Dad had a chicken's head in one hand and an axe in the other – ready to do the deed. One sad look from the bird saw the chickens bundled back in the car and home to where they came from!

"When he was in the station one day a constable was writing a statement and Dad looked over the young man's shoulder and pointed to the word 'enuf'. The P.C. looked up and said, 'Oh yes Sarge, it's double F isn't it'!"

A citation from Braunton Rotary Club in recognition of Ossie's contribution to the community said he was a man of great drive to get things done. When he saw there was no snooker table in the village he found one in Ilfracombe and arranged for it to be moved and installed in the Agricultural Inn. 'Ossie's volunteers' lifted the massive table into place. Later with more friends he founded the Fortescue Club in Wrafton Road and had the table moved there.

He served in the Royal Navy in WWII and in later years he helped set up the Royal Naval Association in Braunton and was very proud of the comradeship this created.

Larger than life, a strong man, a gentle man, a family man, a wonderful friend to many and one who served his community well. A true legend was Ossie Osborn.

In 1970 Ossie and his wife Mary became the licensees of the Mariners Arms in South Street where he was a popular mine host to many sporting clubs.

Barbara tells the story of the evening in May, 1973 when she gave birth to Ossie's first granddaughter. After receiving the phone call Ossie declared the pub was shut and to lock the doors. And a party began!

Much later in the evening customer Bill Ashton was searching for his false teeth which he had mislaid during a visit to the outside convenience. They couldn't be found anywhere.

The neighbourhood soon were aware of the story of the lost teeth! Within a few days a workman at the sewage works at Vellator contacted Bill with the news of some gnashers found in a grid there. After an inspection of the dental furniture Bill decided he wouldn't have to invest in a new set of teeth after all!!

Ossie Osborn died in 1998 at the age of eighty and over 350 people attended his funeral. There was a mix of dignitaries and local bad boys of their time which summed up the type of man Ossie was.

Ossie and Mary Osborn at Buckingham Palace to celebrate the Queen's Golden Wedding Anniversary, 15 July 1997.

Braunton's police staff in the early 1990s. Back Row L-R: PCs Graham Lees, Adrian Pope, Dave James, George Furneaux and Phil Powell. Seated: Enquiry Clerk Shirley Smithers, Sgt Keith Worthington and Traffic Warden Ted Sweeny.

To complete this twentieth-century line up of Braunton's policemen we have Philip Powell who became a police constable in Devon and Cornwall Constaulary in 1975. He moved to Braunton in 1977. Except for the time he spent as Barnstaple town's Community Constable Phil spent all his police years in the service of the people of Braunton and district. Even after he retired Phil worked as the enquiry clerk at the new police station at the back of Caen Street Car Park for another six years until due to financial cuts the decision was made to close this station to the public in 2011.

Police personnel still work from there and cover the large geographical area of the beaches of Saunton, Croyde and Putsborough inland to Marwood, Ashford and Muddiford. We've come a long way since the day Don Hill and his fellow constables slept over the station and had to answer the phone and doorbell at all hours of the day and night!

Phil Powell as enquiry clerk at Braunton Police
Station after completing his police service.

PC Ken Salter who first came to
Braunton in 1934 when he was twelve
as his father was the sergeant in
charge of the village station. Ken
joined the Devon Constabulary but
the war interrupted his service when
he joined the Navy. He later became a
detective with the Devon force.

PC Chris Tucker practising community
liaison by joining the crowds sledging
down a hill above Saunton Park in 2009.

Colin and Brian Clarke – brothers as special police
constables in Braunton.

Chapter 11

Doctors and Nurses

Our longest-living villagers keenly remember medical man Dr Frederick Robert Elliston Wright.

The son of a billiard table manufacturer, he graduated from St Thomas's Hospital in London in 1904 and became a top eye surgeon there.

During his years at St Thomas's he had fallen in love with Josephine Harper who was an ophthalmic ward sister. She was the daughter of Barnstaple surgeon Dr Joseph Harper and they lived at Heanton Punchardon.

When Josephine's brother Dr Walter Harper came to see her at the hospital he not only invited Elliston to visit him at his home, West Mead in Braunton but

Dr Ellison Wright cuts the ribbon to open Leslie Moon's new shop at West Cross.

also offered him a partnership. In 1907 Elliston took him up on this offer and also married Josephine.

The couple settled in with Walter at West Mead which today is the Leonard Cheshire Home, until they moved to Sharland House in 1912.

Dr Wright is remembered for his direct way of speaking to people and for his purposeful stride which caused his long raincoat to swing about his legs. He was a man with a foot in two different worlds, although they were bound together by science. A man who specialised in the eyes and whose other main interest was botany and natural history.

Braunton Burrows in its pre-military and pre-tourist days was a haven of wild life. Dr Wright wrote many papers and books on his subject. He was always ready to discuss, dissect and explain about any plant, bird or bug his patients took to him. It was said he would give them more information about these than about their health!

It is said that if he wasn't in the mood for his surgery he would peer around the waiting room door and look to see who was there, then pick up his stick and stride off muttering that, "it was all a waste of time!"

However, the locals took him and his off-beat ways to their hearts, and it must be said that he was a man of his people and enjoyed joining in their pursuits such as the football club and the skittles team at the Mariners Arms. He also loved to go out with the ships from Vellator and was a shareholder in several of them. As often as he could he took working holidays so he could accompany them on one of their trips around the coast. Lundy Island was a favourite and he would often stay there and study the plant life. It was there that he discovered the Lundy Cabbage which only grew on the island and it was named after him – Brassicella Wrightii.

When Dr Wright first came to Braunton he would travel everywhere on horse-back. Later he took to a bicycle which was replaced by a motorbike. However, in 1942 disaster struck, or should one say an RAF vehicle struck him, near Heanton Court, breaking his leg. After this accident Bert Braund drove him everywhere in his taxi. A great friendship developed between the two, which lasted for twenty years or more.

Josephine died in 1957 and Elliston nine years later. In the *General Medical Journal* of August 1966 Dr.

Left: *Dr Alex and Mrs Barbara Traill and their daughter Jean at Downend in 1930.*
Above: *Dr Traill and Jean 1928.*

Wright's partner Dr John Ritchie wrote that "He was a clinician of the old school, who learned to diagnose without the aids of the modern laboratory. His prognoses were uncannily correct, the result of years of experience and observation. It was not for medicine only that he was remembered, but for his contribution to natural science, and for his great character."

The obituary continued, "He was an authority on Braunton Burrows and naturalists from many countries sought his help and advice." And finished with, "He worked and lived for his community for over sixty years and his passing marks the end an era, a great era of real old gentlemanly doctors who, with the parsons, tended to the needs of their community. I had the honour to be his partner for a quarter of a century, and found him a delightful colleague and friend, kindly, courteous and full of absolute integrity".

In the early years Dr Wright's partner had been Dr Alexander Kirk Traill and their surgery was at the bottom of Heanton Street next to the Railway Inn.

On her yearly visit to her childhood home I met Jean Traill, Dr Traill's daughter and she told me about her life in the village until she left to become a physiotherapist.

Jean was born at their home, Broadlands in Lower Park Road, in 1927. By then there were three partners in the medical practice. Jean recalls that each day her father had two surgeries and in between times he would drive around the countryside to visit patients. If he was going near any of the beaches he would take her and her half-sister Ursula with their nanny and they would play on the sands.

In November, 1934 the family moved further along the road to house called Tyspane.

During the war petrol was rationed but doctors had a plentiful supply. When her father's partner, Dr Ritchie, went on his rounds she would go with him and he would give her driving lessons on the way back. She became the proud owner of a driving licence at the age of just sixteen. (Driving tests were only resumed until after the war ended.)

Alick Traill is remembered as a kindly, friendly physician who was the doctor who delivered Braunton's babies that arrived during the night hours.

His health deteriorated and in 1944 he became seriously ill with angina. He had had several heart attacks and farmers had to pull his car out of ditches but he always swore them to secrecy as he didn't want his wife worried. Eventually he had to go into a nursing home and died aged seventy, in 1945.

Trained at King's College Hospital, Dr John Ritchie joined doctors Wright and Traill in their practice in 1938. He hailed from Anglesey and this was his first post as a General Practioner.

When Joy Hill was six in 1938 Dr John Ritchie came to live with them at Ashcroft, Barton Lane, and it was nineteen years later when he left their house to get married.

Joy said Dr Traill came to see her mother to ask if the new G.P. who was joining their practice could lodge with them.

Joy's mother told the family, "I've said we'll have him – but you won't like him." "But I did, right from the first moment he came to the house," Joy told me.

When Joy was eight she had her tonsils out and during her convalescence the doctor would take her out with him on his rounds in his Sunbeam Talbot.

She would wait in his car whilst he visited his patients. On one occasion he was visiting a titled lady who lived at Woolacombe. After a while the doctor came out and told Joy to follow him into the house as they were being invited to take coffee.

Reluctantly Joy trailed in after the doctor fully expecting to find her ladyship dripping in gold and diamonds! On the way home the doctor stopped the car and told her that she was 'never to do that again'. Thinking that she had spoken out of turn or showed him up with bad manners she remonstrated that she hadn't done anything wrong. But the doctor said she was never to allow herself to be intimidated by anyone ever again. He explained that her family were the salt of the earth and she was as good as anyone.

Joy assured me she has lived all her life by this sound advice. Her father had thought the world of John Ritchie and always called him 'The Boy'. Joy thinks it was because the doctor was the same age as Walter's son Frank who died when he was only nine.

When the doctor went out of an evening to a dinner

party or to meet friends her father would always wait up for him and go and unlock the back gate so he could drive in.

The family had a white Persian cat who was always making off on his nefarious activities which meant the family were often out on search parties before bedtime. Joy recalled the evening when the doctor returned home after visiting friends. Seeing the usual sight of an escaping white cat making a bolt for freedom, the doctor in his evening attire chased after it down Wellclose Road. Once he had caught and returned it to the family sanctuary he was told he'd brought home the wrong cat!

Dr John Ritchie gives Joy Hill away at her wedding.

Joy said that Dr Ritchie was well thought of in the village and she knew how much he valued his patients. He would often bring home his worries about a patient and study medical books late into the night or phone other medics to consult them on difficult diagnoses.

He always referred to Braunton as his home and Joy's family as his family and would tell visiting friends that he lived with the family and not the other way about.

After their parents died Dr Ritchie gave away Joy and her two sisters at their weddings.

John Ritchie's daughter, Professor Jean Crabtree, told me that her father had known her mother Patricia since he played rugby with her brother when they were all growing up in South Wales. Patricia and her cousin met one of the doctor's patients while visiting friends in Braunton. The patient made it her business to act as matchmaker and paid a visit to the surgery and told him where Patricia was staying. The rest is history as they say!

When John and Patricia married they lived in Little Orchard in Higher Park Road, where his only daughter, Jean, was born and later they moved to Portaway where they remained for the rest of their lives and which Jean still owns.

Nurses

Christine Dymond, who lived with her brother Ron and parents

Christine Chapple State Registered Nurse in 1968.

Art and Evelyn Chapple in Exeter Road, became a nursing student at the North Devon Infirmary at Barnstaple. She said she used to catch the 6.50am bus at Braunton and be on duty by 7.30am ready to start work in the Diet Kitchen.

When she had moved into the Nurses Home Christine had to conform to the rules of the matron and be in by 10pm. Along with the other nurses she was very happy when a new matron gave students their own keys. No longer did they have to climb in through the downstairs windows when they returned after the front door had been locked.

Christine became a State Registered Nurse in 1968, the same year as she married Jeffrey Dymond at St Brannocks church.

She became a School Nursing Sister, covering primary schools all over North Devon. Later the area was split into five areas, Ilfracombe, Braunton, Barnstaple, South Molton and Bideford. Christine became responsible for the Braunton section.

Whilst at Caen Street School, a project was suggested to involve the children in such a way as to prevent any nervousness if they had to go into hospital.

Christine and teacher Jean Waldron turned the classrooms into different departments of a hospital. There were wards, X-ray department, operating theatre, a hospital café and other equipment, such as stethoscopes, bandages, masks and gloves.

The hospital co-operated with a video of two children going into hospital, one for an operation and the other for tests. Two nursing sisters became actresses for a day, playing the part of mothers. Christine wrote a poem and the children enacted it at one of their assemblies.

Afterwards the children were encouraged to ask questions and their parents felt they had learnt a great deal from the activities in which the children had taken part.

St John Ambulance

Pam Munt joined Braunton's St John Ambulance in 1957 when she was eight. In fact, she had

Pupils of Caen Street School who acted out being in hospital.

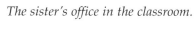

The sister's office in the classroom.

Pam Page receives her Grand Prior Award from Area Superintendent Miss Valentine.

St John's Ambulance Nurses late 1930s. Back Row L-R: Gwen Page, Florence Ackland, Miss Valentine, Alice Page, Mrs Mock. Middle row: Mabel Lamprey, unknown, Evelyn Petherick, Sylvia Welch and Mrs Watts. Front row: Nancy Lane, Mrs Incledon, Mrs Montaque and Dorothy Rogers.

Trophy winners. Standing: *Gwen Page, Morwenna Incledon and Mary Watts.* Seated: *Phyllis Barnet and Margaret Bates.*

On parade by St Brannock's church.

Miss Felicity Valentine opens the new St John Ambulance HQ at Heanton Street in the early 1960s. Escott Scoines and the Bishop of Exeter look on.

The St John Ambulance nurses who manned the ambulances service up until 1972, L-R: Gwen Page, Phyllis Barnett, Marjorie Tucker, Christine Goodwin, Faye Pickard, Mrs Rogettes, Pam Page, Christine Crocker, Kathleen Goodyear, Winnie Knight and Alice Evans.

Left: Superintendent Joe Shute. At his retirement in 1968.

retirement and now runs the Georgeham School St John Ambulance Badger Group with the five to ten year olds.

Today the St John Ambulance meets in St Brannock's Church Rooms as their headquarters, which were in Heanton Street from the early 1960s, are up for sale. Originally the group used to meet in rooms that stood on the Council car park beside the library.

Up until the 1972 the St John Ambulance Brigade was the only ambulance service and was run entirely by volunteers. Pam told me that a phone call for an ambulance came through to the home of whoever was on duty and they would summon whoever else was needed. It was mainly women who undertook the daytime duties as the men were at work and the men would take over at night but if a nurse was required she would have to be picked up en route.

Hilary Edmonds' father Joe Shute served with the brigade for thirty-four years and was for many years a Superintendent with St John Ambulance in Braunton. She recalls that as the ambulance service was completely reliant on donations to keep it running, many of the group would make collections on Sundays by fixing sheets out along the Braunton road and passers-by would throw their money into it.

been going along to meetings, competitions and events since she was a babe in arms as her father, his brother and two sisters and a sister-in-law were all lifetime members.

Pam has been associated with the brigade all her life working her way up to County Recruitment Officer until the end of 2013 when she took semi-

Chapter 12
Churches

St Brannock's Parish Church

Braunton's parish church is no longer in the centre of the village as it was in times past. As the village expanded and moved closer to the Great Field and to Braunton Pill when shipping became important, the church was left on the edge of the settlement and today sits beside Chaloners Road.

It is thought that the church was built at the latter end of the thirteenth century, although a place of worship has stood on the site since AD550 when Braunton's patron saint St Brannock built a Christian church.

Legend has it that St Brannock attempted to build on a hilltop overlooking the village. However, it kept collapsing. In a dream, he was told to look for a sow and her piglets beside a stream and this would be the site. The church today stands on the field where St Brannock's dream came true!

This story is depicted on a stained glass window and one of the many excellently carved and painted roof bosses. The story of St Brannock is also told on some of the many intricately carved pew ends.

The tower with its lead-covered timber octagonal spire is one of only three in North Devon. The other two are at Barnstaple and Swimbridge and all three suffer from distortion due to the heat of the sun. The lead on the spire is interestingly laid in diagonal strips which shine in the sunlight and may well have come from Combe Martin where there were lead mines.

The bell tower holds eight bells at least six of them founded or recast by Taylor and Sons of Loughborough.

Inside St Brannock's church.

St Brannock's church.

Margaret Clarke who was born in 1890, was the daughter of Church Street's blacksmith John Elliott. In her memoirs she said her father was a great churchman and had a very powerful base voice, which was much admired. He also looked after the church clock and the peal of bells. And being the eldest child, Margaret had to go with him up into the tower to hold the lantern when he wound up the clock and while he oiled the bells and tied on the muffler when there was a funeral. She said she didn't like going up into the tower as it was full of bats, which when disturbed would fly all around her.

St Brannock's bell ringers early 1900s – third from left Jocker Smith and far right the blacksmith John Elliott.

She also remembers the Sunday school treat was an exciting day for the children. It started with a flower service in the church when they took bunches of flowers and walked in turn up to the altar and presented them to the vicar. When they came out of church, there in the grove would be horses and carts with bundles of straw laid each side for the children to sit on and the farmers would take them to Saunton Sands, where they paddled and played games. They would then climb up to the 'Lorna Doone Hotel' where Mr and Mrs Slee had prepared a lovely tea for them.

Later they would return to the meadow beside the vicarage and there would be races and games and the grown-ups would listen to the Braunton Brass Band playing. There would also be dancing and even the church bells would be rung.

Returning to the twenty-first century. In the summer of 2003 the church was the victim of a fire that did a million pounds of damage. The repairs left it unable to hold services for eighteen months.

The fire occurred only a few weeks after a great deal of work

Rev. John Henry Prince – Vicar of St Brannock 1916-1946.

Rev. Thomas Arthur Hancock – Vicar of St Brannock's 1946-1952.

had been carried out on the spire and lead and wood had been replaced and strengthened. During the exercise it was found that much of the wood dated back to the thirteenth century and the original church.

Including Saint Brannock, who founded the church in 550, there have been 55 rectors. The most recent incumbency broke with tradition in 2006 when the Reverend Anne Thorne was installed as the first woman priest in this parish church.

Born in Dorset, Anne is mother to Mark and Becky and grandma to six year old George and four year old twins Bria and Noah. Before becoming a priest Anne was an accountant and had her own bookkeeping firm.

Before she came to Braunton she had been at Beer in East Devon for four years and prior to that at The Colleigate Church of the Holy Cross and the Mother of Him Who Hung Thereon – more usually known as Crediton parish church!

Rev. Roger Reeve –Vicar St Brannock's 1978-2006 and Marie and Roy Lucas.

Rev. Anne Thorne, the present Vicar of St Brannock's since 2006.

St Brannock's is a busy parish which Anne loves and when asked what she enjoys most about her work she replied that the highlight of her year was the Christmas Eve Crib Service.

Although the event had been held for many years the 2013 Christmas was the most memorable. There were 681 in the congregation and 250 of these were children, nearly all in nativity costume. The mammoth task of costumier fell to Lindsey Griffin who did a sterling job making outfits for shepherds, kings, angels and everyone else who took part in the nativity story including Father Christmas. Anne said the atmosphere in the church was electric.

St Ann's Chapel

Anne is also pleased that in 2013 the other church in her care St Anne's chapel at Saunton, was licensed for weddings. This is a delightful building which holds the name of another ancient chapel reputed to have stood near the shore on Braunton Burrows opposite Appledore.

The remains of the first St Anne's chapel were still visible in the early 1800s and there was reported to have been several houses in and around it, although all signs of them have now been swallowed up by the sand. Today's St Anne's chapel has an ancient weathered stone basin said to be the font from the original chapel in the dunes.

St Brannoc's

Braunton has two churches dedicated to the saint. On the opposite side of the road from the parish church, hidden among the trees on the hillside is the small Roman Catholic church of St. Brannoc's Well. Only 60 feet long it replaces an ancient church that had fallen into decay by the end of the nineteenth century.

The new church was built as a memorial to the parents of Mrs Angela Incledon-Webber who lived at

Buckland House. The holy well is in the form of a heart-shaped pool and is fed by a spring from the nearby hillside. Today this church is rarely in use as services are held at the church of St. Michael and all Angels at the Royal Marine Barracks, Chivenor.

The Methodist Church

The eighteenth century saw the rise of Methodism after the teachings of John Wesley who held his meetings in the open air. Gradually simple places of worship arose and Braunton's first Methodist church was built in 1833 on Rumsam Close near the top of Heanton Street. But the congregation dwindled and by 1870 there were only a few worshippers left.

With visiting preachers the congregation grew and the fortunes of the church were greatly improved by the late 1880s. At the beginning of the twentieth century the church built two new classrooms and a new entrance. An extension was built to house the choir and a new organ and manse were provided for a resident minister.

In 1981, when the disused Barnstaple to Ilfracombe railway line was released for public use plans were drawn up for a new Methodist church on this ground.

The Methodist church in Hillsview. Now the Elliott Gallery.

The congregation of the Methodist church gathered outside.

The children from the Methodist church c.1908.

The Band of Hope from the Congregational church in 1920s.

A Christmas performance at the Congregational church.

The Congregational Church

From as early as the Act of Uniformity of 1662 the non-conformists of Braunton came together and created the Congregational church in East Street.

While improvements to the seating and pulpit area were carried out in the Congregational church in 1867 the Methodist congregation invited the Congregationalists to join them at their church at the top of Heanton Street.

Further improvements were made by the minister in 1885 when he drew up plans for a new Sunday school to be built beside the church. This opened on Good Friday 1887.

Perhaps this is the place to divulge the adventures of Norman Venner and his friends back in the days of their childhood in the 1940s.

This story involves Miss Geen and her shop at the bottom of Heanton Street. On Sundays when Norman and his mates had to attend morning service they would climb up the back stairs to the balcony and sing the first hymn with gusto. Then as the Rev. Clarke's sermon held little interest for young active minds the boys would slide away from the service and down the stairs to get up to no good.

Sometimes they would collect halfpennies with Britannia's head on and go down to the railway line and place the coins on the rails. By now it was time to make their way back to the chapel to sing the last hymn as if butter wouldn't melt in their mouths!

Next day they would retrace their steps to the scene of the crime and retrieve the halfpennies which with a bit of luck were now twice as large and the size of a penny. The coins would be taken to Miss Geen, who had bad eye sight, and exchanged for a penny's worth of sherbet. Sometimes Miss Geen after feeling the coin all over would send them on their way without coin or sherbet. Perhaps she was wise to their tricks!

Christ Church

In the early 1970s the United Reformed Church was formed when the Congregational Church of England and Wales joined with the Presbyterian Church of England. However, there was no minister at the East Street church for eight years until the Rev. John Ticehurst arrived in 1983.

During this time the Methodists had been contemplating building on the old railway line but after discussions were held between them and the United Reformed church members it was decided that the two churches should come together under one roof. This took place in 1986 when the new modern building of 'Christ Church' was opened next door to the old Congregational church.

The unification of these two religious bodies was skilfully managed by Reverend Amos Cresswell who at the time was the leader of the Plymouth and Exeter Methodist District and by the Moderator Michael Hubbard who was the leader of the United Reform Church for the South West. The Rev. Amos Cresswell is still very much in evidence and a strong supporter at Christ Church twenty-eight years later.

There are two other non-conformist churches in Braunton. One is the Gospel Hall in South Street which was built in 1931, replacing its original Meeting Hall in Heanton Street. It is a free and independent church and a member of the evangelical tradition.

The other is the Coastal Community Church which is of the Pentecostal belief.

One of the Christ Church active supporters is Mike Marshall who has lived in Braunton since he was posted to RAF Chivenor in 1965.

Mike joined the RAF in May 1941. A year later he was posted to join the Sunderland Flying Boats at Pembroke Dock and in 1943 he was drafted to the Far East. The rest of the war Mike served in many different parts of India. The 8 May, 1945 found him celebrating VE Day in Germany. But Mike's war was not over yet as two months later he was on his way to Burma.

Mike's wartime service ended for him in September 1946 but the following year he re-joined the RAF where he remained for another twenty-two years. During this time he married his beloved wife Jinny in 1951 and had three sons Rodney, David and Paul, who have now made Mike a proud grandfather and great grandfather.

When preparing for retirement from the RAF Mike studied to become a teacher – a post he held at Forches Cross Primary School in Barnstaple from

Mike Marshall with his paper sculpture of St Paul's Cathedral.

Mike at home making his sculpture for Christmas 2013.

1971 to his final retirement in 1985.

During his time at training college Mike discovered the art of paper sculpting. He took this into his classroom and would produce nativity displays for the school at Christmas time. When school was over he would take his sculptures to the children's ward at the North Devon Hospital.

Mike was 'discovered' by a London photographer who was staying at his Croyde guest house at the time of Prince Charles and Lady Diana's wedding and asked him to create a sculpture of St Paul's Cathedral to be used for a wedding broadcast.

For many years now Mike has combined his skill and creative talent to produce paper sculptures of religious scenes for display at Christ Church. They take many hours to make from simple ceiling lining paper and glue, and some are life size.

Mike says the pleasure is in the making of the sculptures and seeing people enjoying them.

Christ Church's Rev. Robert Manning with Mike Marshall and his paper sculpture displayed in the church.

Chapter 13

Schools

School and church shared a natural relationship in Braunton's first seat of education – Chaloner's.

The school was established in 1670 with a bequest from St Brannock's vicar the Rev. William Chaloner. It was held on the top floor of the Church House which still stands today in the churchyard with an archway into Church Street.

The Reverend's idea was to educate the poor boys of the parish in the school which was free. The first master was James Penrose who taught reading, writing and arithmetic but he died within the year and his successor William Ley decided to add Latin to the three R's.

In 1690 Arthur Ackland, left land at George Yeate (now Goodgates) to provide funds to pay for education of 12 poor Braunton children. This Ackland's School was now held on the lower floor of the Church House.

Ackland's became a preparatory school and once the boys had learned to read they could graduate to the 'writing school' – Chaloner's.

In 1854 a new school with two classrooms and a playground had been built although the opening of the Barnstaple to Ilfracombe railway line directly behind it in 1874 could not have been a welcome distraction! Today this building is the fire station.

Compulsory education came about by the Education Act of 1870. Chaloner's boarder's fees were set at 25 guineas per annum and weekly boarders paid 10 shillings a week. The age range of pupils was between seven and fifteen years and by 1878 there were 20 boys attending the school.

Pupils who could no longer pay the fees could attend the elementary school in Caen Street which opened in 1873.

By 1924 a new Ilfracombe to Barnstaple road had been cut into the village taking part of the front garden and playground. With a railway behind and a new wide road in the front of the school it is no wonder headmaster Mr Gass had plans drawn up for

Pupils and teachers of Chaloner's School 1934

a new Chaloner's School on Goodgates fields.

Unfortunately the funds were not forthcoming but lesser plans for playing fields and a pavilion to commemorate the school's old boys who had been killed in WWI did go ahead on the Goodgates land and was completed by 1930.

In 1931 there were 55 boys at the school when it was deemed by the school inspectors to be 'unsatisfactory as a Secondary School' as it needed more staff, more classrooms and more money.

The County Education Committee withdrew all grants to the school in 1933 which was a shock to the village as many boys finished their education at Chaloner's so they had the kudos of being an Old Chalonerian!

When the American Army moved into Braunton to train for the D-Day Landings in France the Goodgates playing field was requisitioned by the War Office for the encampment of these troops.

The playing field and pavilion were sold in the late 1960s to build a housing estate to accommodate the ever growing population of the village.

There are a few school-time memories of those last few years before Chaloner's closed. Farmer's son John Avery attended Caen Street School for the first few years of his education after which he should have gone to the Secondary School but along with a few other boys, his parents sent him to the fee paying Chaloner's. There were two teachers and the Rev. Prince would occasionally attend the school and try unsuccessfully to teach them Latin!

It was wartime and 15 evacuees from London who were living in Ilfracombe travelled to Braunton by train to school. John said their teacher Mr Sparks was the most morose man you could ever meet.

Irene Therin's brother John received a scholarship to Chaloner's during the war after their father Bill Trute was killed in action whilst serving with the Royal Artillery in France. A memory of John's time at the school was the hard and fast rule that the boys were never to be seen outside school without their Chaloner's caps on. It was an ever-lasting call around their home, 'Where's my cap?' In the end he had two caps so there was a greater chance of finding one of them!

Butcher Tony Reed joined the school when he was five. Woe-betide anyone he recalls who was seen out without their cap on.

Chaloner's was run on a charitable status and the charity is still on-going today and Tony is one of its trustees. The trust gives grants twice a year for educational books and equipment.

Religion and education came together in another school in Braunton at the beginning of the twentieth century. A school with a name that bewildered me for some time was the Abertawe School in East Street.

Chaloner's School cap and scarf belonging to Peter Welch.

Built as Chaloner's School in 1854, now Braunton's Fire Station.

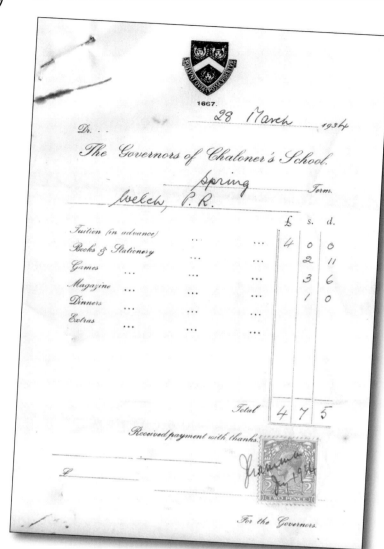

Mr Minchington, Head Master of Caen Street School 1902-1934.

An account for the fees for Chaloner's School for Peter Welch in 1934.

Caen Street School children 1925.

The class of 1928. Back row L-R: *E.Chillcott, J. Holmes, C. Ley, H. Ellis, N. Ashton, W. Packer, E. Thorne, E. West.* 2nd Row: *F. Geen, M. Clarke, F. Mackay, B. Ackland, W. Harris, O. Watts, E. May, V. Crick, F. Clarke, M. Coates.* 3rd Row: *F. Mitchell, F. Symons, M. Lane, E. Sussex, V. Watts, N. Lane, K. Jenkins.* Sitting: *B. Ley, D. Butler, J. Bulled, R. Williams, F. Squires, E. Prince and G. Smale.*

Caen Street nine year olds in 1948. Back Row L-R: *Tony Reed, Stuart Forsyth, Norman James, Glenis Martin, Eileen Williams, Pat Harvey, Enid Lamprey, Angela ? Maureen Wheaton.* 3rd Row: *Margaret Easton, John Slee, Margaret Jenkins, Rea Bradley, Richard Squires, Graham Fisher, Phillip Harris, Norman Venner, Margaret Phillips, Julia Avery and Di Parkhouse.* 2nd Row: *Bill Paul, Raymond Tossell, Bill Mitchell, John Brayley, Ted Brayley, John Clarke, Jean Baglole, Jen Clayton, Irene Trute, Jillian Mitchell.* Front Row: *unknown, Gloria Jones, Brenda Sandecock, Margaret Ballerd, Roy Williams, unknown, Jenny Harris and Graham Osbourne.*

Research informs that Aber is the Welsh prefix for river, so we have the River Taw School. This was held in the Congregational church schoolroom and run by Miss Davies who was the sister of a former minister of the church.

The Abertawe School closed in 1936 and the pupils moved to Chaloner's School.

Until the Education Act of 1870 there were small fee paying schools held in households in several streets in the village wherever there was someone who was educated enough to teach children the three R's.

Tony Reed ready for his school day in his Chaloner's uniform.

After the Act, Board Schools were built country-wide and Braunton's was Caen Street School, built in 1873. To see the school today from the front it looks remarkably as it did when it was first built.

Education was for all children up to the age of fourteen and was supposed to be free to all. However, Braunton children had to pay 1d a week for their schooling. This was a problem for poorer parents with several children. Boys worked in the fields and at Vellator when the ships had to be unloaded. This work helped put food on the table and paid the school fees.

School inspectors reported that the younger pupils' education standards were acceptable but as the children got to an age where they could supplement the family income, their general education standard was poor.

Another reason for absence at this time was illness. There were no inoculations against childhood diseases such as measles, whooping cough and mumps or the more serious illness of diphtheria, scarlet fever and even smallpox. Whenever the school was hit by these diseases it would have to close for several weeks.

Overcrowding, poor heating, ventilation and sanitation seemed to be a problem for many of the early years of the school. But in 1900 a new heating system was reported to have improved the progress, discipline and instruction of the pupils. And after a report by the sanitary inspector in 1914 flushing water closets were installed. In the same year electricity was installed in the classrooms from the newly opened Braunton Electric Light Company.

In 1924 the school was reorganised into Senior and Junior departments as well as the infants and juniors

Caen Street Senior Class 1952/3. Back Row: *unknown, Rodney Standen, Maurice Jenkins, John Lakerman, Christopher Mitchell, Norman Woodley, unknown, Jeffrey Dymond and John Owen.* 2nd Row: *June Lamprey, Susan Brent, Susan Williams, ? Passmore, Maureen Bowerman, Janet Waldron, unknown, unknown, Jennifer Welch.* 3rd Row: *Alison Selway, unknown, unknown, unknown, Shelia Rook, Geraldine Baker, ? Clarke.* Front Row: *Robert Gibbs, unknown, Maurice Clements, Richard Whittington, Lawrence Lamprey and Timothy Harvard.*

being mixed boys and girls. A report in the following year shows that there were up to 50 pupils to a class, in rooms that were too small. However, there was 'great satisfaction' in the scholars' work that year and they were well behaved and orderly!

Brian Williams recalls his first day at Caen Street School in 1935 when his teacher eventually detached his fingers from the school door handle and introduced herself as Miss Thorne and reassured him that she was sure they would get along well together.

She was a timeless lady whose gentle and generous nature inspired trust and comfort says Brian. Tall and invariably clad in long flowing dresses of pastel shades and broad brimmed hats, Miss Thorne had no difficulty in keeping 40 or more five and six year olds in a happy state of contentment. However, the following year Brian's teacher was Miss Reeves, a no-nonsense, back-to-basics type, who was quick to tell Brian he was 'A stupid boy'.

It was in these early school days that Brian earned the name of Pussy! This came about because the children were sent on a nature walk and told to come back with an interesting twig or flower. Brian returned with a piece of Pussy Willow and when Miss Reeves asked him what it was he replied "Dunno Miss, but it's soft and fluffy." And as children love alliteration he was soon being called Pussy Willow Williams which was shortened to Pussy.

Now in his eightieth decade and with an impressive record of teaching in Barnstaple Grammar School, British Forces Schools in Cyprus and Singapore and headships in other parts of England and a lifelong involvement on the rugby field Brian is still hailed as 'Pussy' by everyone who knows him.

John Avery who lived at South Dene Farm, recalls his first day at school in Caen Street in 1938. He was supposed to have gone to West Down School as he was in their catchment area but his mother thought it too dangerous for her four year old son to walk along the main road to West Down. So John was among 50/60 children from outlying areas who went by bus to Caen Street School.

John remembers that he found the school children extremely rough and boisterous. He recalled that the teacher Miss Clark seemed to be afraid of the pupils and could not control them. John said that on more than one occasion he was so scared he just walked out of school and walked home.

Since 1907 gardening had been taught to the boys on a piece of land next to the school. Dorothy Davies said her brother Sam loved these lessons and when in 1937 the Senior School opened in Barton Lane he helped move the equipment and chicken sheds to the newly opened school.

Caen Street School was the first port of call in Bill Mitchell's venture into education and in 1939 at the age of eleven and at the onset of WWII he transferred to the newly built Braunton Senior School. His

Caen Street Netball Team 1957 – Gillian Goodliffe, Pat Slade, Diane Featherstone, unknown. **Sitting:** *Ruth Bedford unknown, unknown.*

Fancy dress.

Maypole dancing at the Centenary Celebrations at Caen Street School in 1973.

Pupils who left Caen Street School in 1988. Back Row L-R: *Brian Davis, Robert Huxtable, Roger Lamprey, Michael Davis, David Holman, Keith Franks, Anthony St. John, Peter Durrant and Jon Jarvis.* 2nd Row: *Jacqueline Davis, Lesley Bater, Lynn West, Carole Reees, Marilyn Abbott, Jennifer Davies, Shelia Jones, Geraldine Tremaine, Avril Smale and Jean Cranch.* 3rd Row: *Ann Woodley, Jacqueline Wensley, Shelia Broadbridge, Ann Slack, Brenda Dimbleby, Suzanne Williams, Pamela Raby, Jane Toogood and Christine Chapple.* Sitting: *Jeffrey Williams, Peter Smaldon, unknown, Terry Patchett, unknown, unknown, unknown, Tony Hoile and unknown.*

The official key presented to the Senior School when it opened in 1937.

The entrance to the Senior School in Barton Road.

The inner quadrangle of the school.

Note the open corridors open to all winds and weather. Now they are enclosed with windows.

abiding memory of this new venture was going off on his first day with his newly acquired gas mask on his back. Within six months the school was full with up to 40 or 50 pupils to each class due to an influx of wartime evacuees.

For those boys who did not seem academically inclined the headmaster had plans to help the war effort by getting them to 'Dig for Victory'. There was a 2 acre field at the top of Lower Park Road where the boys were put to work weeding between the lines of potatoes. They were told that at the bottom of the field there was lemonade for those who finished weeding! But if the German aircraft came over they were to run for cover in the woods!!

Bill also recalled when Mr Babb the Headmaster called him to one side and told him to go to the garden opposite the school – now Southmead School – and pick the best cauliflower he could find and then take it to his home for his wife to cook for dinner. So it is with little wonder that in 1942 a fortnight before he was due to leave school Bill went to the Head and asked if he could leave school early to go to sea on his father's boat. The teachers reply was that as he didn't seem to be learning anything he may as well go. This was not entirely correct of course as he certainly knew how to till a garden!

John Prior, who lived at the London Inn in Caen Street, only had to cross the road to go to school during those war years. His mother also, as she became a teacher there. John's memory of school at this time was when their favourite teacher Mr Richardson, who had a great passion for nature study, was killed in action. John recalls that the teacher's family set up a fund from which each year a grant would be awarded to the pupil who excelled as a naturalist.

John's mother Audrey also taught at Heanton and Ashford Primary School during the war years. Built in 1877, it catered for the children of the farming community. Unfortunately the facilities improved very little over the next hundred years as there was only one flushing toilet for the teachers and the children had to make do with earth closets.

The school closed in 1958. One of Braunton's daughters Iva Keast was the youngest of six children of Richard and Betsy Williams of Williams Shoe Shop at 5, South Street. Iva was born in 1904, a bright child who became the head girl of Barnstaple Girls Grammar School and won a scholarship to Exeter University.

In the meantime the Caen Street School building was becoming more and more dilapidated and there

Pupils of Heanton School in the last term before the school closed in 1958. Back Row: *Pamela Joslin, Colin Spear, Richard Harding, Alan Gammon, Jeffrey Thatcher, Michael Johns and Marilyn Allen.* 2nd Row: *Stephen Bedford, Andrew Woods, Judith Woods, Adrian Hill, Heather Spear, Bobby Thatcher, Julie Cuthbutson, Christine Harris and Jane Wood.* 3rd Row: *Joyce Bedford, Pauline Joslin, Kathleen Manning, Susan Pugsley, Janet Piper and Shirley Barrow.* 4th Row: *Pat Piper, Ian Cuthbutson, Barry Manning, Pam Pace, Ian Pugsley, Alan Bedford and Denise Pugsley.* Front Row: *Michael Challacombe, Raymond Dymond, Roger Dymond and Graham Harris.*
Teachers: *Mrs Iva Keast* (on the left) *and Headmaster Mr R. Curtis* (on the right).

was a great need for repair and expansion. This took place in the 1960s but the cooked dinners were still being prepared elsewhere and delivered to the 250 children who partook of them daily. It wasn't until 1972 that the school had their own kitchens. And due to various fund raising events, by the time the school was celebrating its centenary in 1973 it could boast its own swimming pool.

One thing that stayed the same for all the pupils of Caen Street School from the time it was built in 1873 until 2013. That was the Horse Chestnut tree which stood by the entrance gates for at least 114 years. Unfortunately due to disease this grand old dame had to be laid to rest before the children returned after the summer holidays.

Headmaster of Caen Street School Mr Babb became the first Headmaster of a newly built Senior School. The register opened in August, 1937 with 150 pupils. All of them had local addresses in Braunton and the surrounding area except for the coastguard's son whose last school was in Frazerburgh, Scotland! By September 1939 there were 124 new pupils of whom 57 were evacuees and came from many London boroughs. Another 66 evacuees arrived at the school in the following year. You might think that the school would be bursting at the seams but many of these children returned home again within days or weeks. This migration continued for the rest of the war.

By the 1950s the register returns to

Headmaster 1953-1957, Maurice Bound.

the intake from local schools and children of servicemen at RAF Chivenor.

My thanks to Braunton Academy for allowing me sight of this register for the research for this book. Every leaf in it is a page of history not yet told.

Maurice Bound was Headmaster of Braunton Secondary Modern School between 1951-57 and remembers his time there with the greatest of pleasure and satisfaction. To mark his one hundredth birthday in 2013 the administrator Judy Nolan collected photographs and memorabilia of the era when Mr Bound held the reins of the scholastic wagon which was then called Braunton Secondary Modern School.

In a letter of thanks Maurice Bound said he remembered the family atmosphere fostered at the school by the staff and that they concentrated on educating the 'whole child'.

Since 1937 Braunton's Senior School has gone through all the name changes and now is an Academy which benefits from greater freedoms from the local authority and is able to choose its own curriculum. It can also set its own pay and conditions for the staff and determine the length of the school days and term times.

From times when it was rare for children to have the opportunity to pass exams and enter higher education, the students at Braunton Academy have forged a pathway for others to follow. Head Boy in 2008, Aydan Greatrick secured a place at Selwyn College,

Christmas Cake Competition at the Senior School in 1955.

Braunton Comprehensive School 1978 with all the students that were leaving that year.

Cambridge to read history. He has now set up a Uni-Club to encourage other Braunton students to aim for places at the world's finest universities. Aydan also arranged a link between his university and the Academy's history department.

Harry Hall and Joe Cammack have also obtained scholarships to study GCE 'A' Level at Eton College.

Joe Cammack who won a scholarship to Eton College in 2010.

As the village expanded at a record speed two more primary schools were built over the next twenty years. Southmead School was built in 1968. Today, due to its closeness to the Royal Marine Base at Chivenor many of its pupils are from service families.

Kingsacre School was built in 1983 on the housing estate alongside the Saunton Road. It took many of the extra children who had arrived in the village due to the reopening of RAF Chivenor in 1980.

This should be where our chapter ends but there is one more school to mention – Mrs Traill's Scarlet Runners!

When Dr Alexander Traill met and married Barbara Godby their first house in Braunton was Broadlands in Lower Park Road and their daughter Jean was born there in January 1927.

Dr and Mrs. Traill lived the life of times gone by. Days of cooks, maids, gardeners, nannies and governesses. Of garden parties, cocktails and dinner parties.

It was at one of Mrs Traill's bridge parties that a friend asked if her granddaughter could come and live with them and share Jean's nanny.

Ann whose parents were in Malaya, was two years younger than Jean and the two girls spent all their time together until they went to boarding school. The girls were always dressed alike in clothes that the Traill's nanny made.

Jean recalls that when both girls caught whooping cough they were packed off with nanny to live in the Traill's beach hut at Saunton Sands to recuperate. Tough love!!

Aerial view of the Senior School and Southmead School.

Tyspane in 1934 – the original house as it was when the Traills bought it.

Aerial view of the Brittons estate when it was being built. Tyspane is the house standing in its own grounds on the centre right. Note the Bowling Club in front of it and slightly to the left.

The Scarlet Runners on a winter walk.

At a summer fête.

The children in the garden at Tyspane with nanny.

Playing in the garden at Tyspane in the 1930s.

In 1934 Barbara Traill announced to the family that they were moving to a larger house called Tyspane in Lower Park Road.

There were many rooms for servants and staff and the views from the large front windows were over to the Taw and Torridge estuary.

When they first moved to Tyspane Jean says there were only four children but soon they were joined by another family of four and a resident governess, Miss Hodges, who although a very good teacher was very strict. There were lessons all morning and nature walks in the afternoon and then further lessons after tea.

By the time WWII started there were 16 children boarding and being schooled at Tyspane and by 1946 there were 21 with a large staff. Jean says there was always plenty of children to play with even when some of them went home in the holidays, there was always seven or eight who lived with them permanently.

The children were all given little basket suitcases to keep their personal belongings in. And Mrs Traill had scarlet knitted jerseys made for all the pupils so that they could be easily identified when they were away from Tyspane. This gave them the name of Mrs Traill's Scarlet Runners (as in runner beans!)

Jean says her mother was not a business woman and would welcome another child who might be with them for a few months or even ten years. The children came to the school for many different reasons, divorce or death of a parent but usually the parents were posted to the Far East with the military or the Diplomatic Corps and were away for as much as four years. The children were guaranteed a comprehensive education from Miss Hodges. Teachers also came in from the village to teach dancing and the children went next door for piano lessons and twice a week they went horse riding.

During the war years the gardens at Tyspane were put to good use providing fruit and vegetables for the household which by 1944 had swelled to 30 people. Barbara Traill would take all the children's ration books around the shops in the village to try and find extra food for the household. And in case of invasion Mrs Traill had an organised plan to take all the children to a cave she had found along one of the country lanes.

Just months before the end of the war Dr Traill died but his wife continued with the school. Jean was waiting to start her training in a London hospital as a physiotherapist but in the meantime took a job in a solicitor's office in Braunton.

On finishing her training in 1947 Jean married and worked in the Barnstaple and Ilfracombe hospitals as a physiotherapist.

The number of pupils at Tyspane eased by 1951 when there were still 18 boarders. Barbara Traill died in 1957 and although Jean now married with three sons and living in Holland did consider running the school but it was not possible and so Tyspane was sold.

Dr Ritchie's daughter Jean Crabtree recalls that she went to school at Tyspane between 1957-61 when the headmaster was Mr Riddell and whilst her parents went away on holiday she would also board at the school.

The house became a Nursing Home in 1986 after many years of being the home of the Scarlet Runners.

The Wedding of Mike and Ann Inglis in 1948 at St Brannock's church with a guard of honour by the Scarlet Runners. Ann was the first child to be taken under the wings of the Traills at Tyspane. She met Mike when he was posted to the area after the war in charge of clearing all the mines from the beaches.

Chapter 14

Sporting Clubs

Braunton Association Football Club

Sir Francis Drake came ashore at Vellator and climbed West Hill to view a vista he declared as "The finest I've seen in all of Europe."

Legend of course. But not to the football-loving Braunton players who took on the nickname of 'The Men of Drake'.

John Clarke who started playing football on Braunton's recreation ground in the 1940s gave me the story of Braunton's football history.

The North Devon League formed in 1904 by Braunton, Bideford, South Molton, Barnstaple YMCA and Pilton Social Club.

The first match played involving the member clubs was a friendly between Pilton and Braunton which the Men of Drake won by a glorious 4 – 0.

Braunton completed that first season in the newly formed league in third spot. They had to wait until season 1968-69 before claiming the championship crown for the first time in their history.

For a number of years the Recreation Ground on Exeter Road was the home of Braunton Football Club.

John Clarke and Robert Hancock in a training session with the player-manager of Barnstaple Football Club on the Recreation Ground in 1950.

In the early post war years the away team would change at the White Lion Public House and the Braunton players would use Smokey Joe's Café in South Street. The home team later moved 'up market' to the skittle alley at the Mariners Arms Public House. In the late 1950s early 1960s changing rooms were built on the Recreation Grounds.

From around the late 1940s to the mid 1950s Braunton Football Club gained a reputation for providing players to the Devon County senior side on a regular basis. A number of Brauntonians donned the famous green and white shirt – Frank Irwin, Nobby Clark, Les Coates to name a few.

The Westward Ho! tournament acclaimed as the oldest and most popular knock-out in North Devon, was dominated by the 'big three': Bideford Barnstaple, and Ilfracombe.

Braunton reached the final for the first time in 1948 when they played Barnstaple at Barnstaple Rugby Ground. The home team won 5-2 in front of 5000 spectators. Gerald Coates scored both of Braunton's goals.

Four years later and the Men of Drake, reached the final again. Ilfracombe Town provided the opposition and were too strong for the minnows of the North Devon League and claimed the trophy with a 2-0 victory. The Braunton line-up was: J. Brend, C. Mock, R. Brown, G. Coates, F. Irwin, S. Ley, C. Lamprey, R. Clarke, L. Coates, R. Birrell, G. Shaddick.

There were great celebrations when Braunton lifted the Westward Ho! Cup for the first time. In the 50th final they defeated Holsworthy 2-1.

For decades the team sheets were filled with the names of Irwin, Coates, Lamprey and Perryman, along with other families who had lived in Braunton for generations. But in the late 1950s things were to change for the Men of Drake.

Players were drafted in from the nearby RAF Chivenor. Although the servicemen were members of the North Devon Football League, the powers that be sanctioned a move to allow RAF personnel to play for teams outside of the camp limits.

The trend continued into the early 1960s and by then the majority of the Braunton team were from outside the village. The team that won the Torridge Cup in 1965 boasted just two Brauntonians – John Clarke and Sid Windsor.

By the end of the 1982-83 campaign the club known

An early twentieth-century photo of Braunton football team. (Sorry no names. Photograph given to me by Margaret Dent née Atkins.)

The 1920 football team – Henry Mitchell with the ball.

The Westward Ho! Cup Final the 1951-52 season. This game was played on Barnstaple Rugby Ground as it was larger than the football ground. The final used to draw a crowd of 6/7000 people. This match Braunton lost to Ilfracombe Town 2-0. The Westward Ho! Cup is still played for today but on Barnstaple Football Ground. Back row L-R: Charlie Mock, Ernie Brown, John Brend, Cyril Lamprey, Reg Birrell and Gerald Coates. Front row: 'Nobby' Clarke, Ernie Shaddick, Frank Irwin, Les Coates and 'Shaver' Ley. Mascot: Trevor Clark.

Braunton Football Club Committee 1950. L-R: Jack Moore, Bill Coates, Gerald Mace, Jimmy Feetch, Les Baglole, Bill Avery, Sid Ives, Frank Irwin, Dr Ritchie, 'Fanny' Rowlands, Reg Clarke (new Chairman), Ernie Brown, 'Nobby' Clarke, Mervyn Mitchell (Secretary) and Wilf Incledon.

1962/3 Season. The names of the Braunton team who are wearing shirts with dark collars are:- Back Row L-R: *John Fry (Referee) Malcolm Peterson, Bobby Irwin, Michael Perryman, Donald Mitchell, John Clarke, Chris Skelton, Eddie O'Neill and Ron Churchward.* Front row: *John Gubb, Eddie Chichester and 'Taffy' Jenkins.*

as Braunton Association Football Club disbanded. We had to wait until 1987 before the club reformed.

In the early 1990s it was rumoured that Braunton A.F.C. were seriously considering an application for membership to the Western Football League but this did not come to fruition.

Mark Harris who has been involved with the club since a young lad completes the story in saying that Braunton's football matches moved to its present home at Lobb Fields in about 2000, and with grants from several different organisations, changing rooms were built on the ground in 2006.

However, the game of football has never left the village Recreation Ground and now the original changing rooms are being refurbished with a grant from North Devon Council.

Today Braunton is at the top of the North Devon Premier League and their reserves are top of the Senior League.

Braunton Cricket Club

Long-time member, supporter, captain, umpire and president of Braunton Cricket Club, John Fry began his relationship with the club when he went to work for Wilfred and Leslie Moon in their shop on the corner of North Street as a grocer's assistant.

John loved cricket and had joined Braunton, but his employer was not interested in sport and so John had no chance of a Saturday afternoon off to play.

When John married his wife Joan they lived in North Street and when he got a job at the Co-op back in his native Barnstaple he had Saturdays free. Although he was asked to switch his allegiance to Barnstaple Cricket Club he continued to play his favourite game for his favourite club, Braunton.

He was wicket keeper for their first XI and captained the team in 1961 and 1962. Later he formed the second XI and captained that for four years. He then became an umpire not only locally but throughout the County. As president of the club he follows such names as Dr J. Ritchie, Lt Col Ingleton-Webber, Mr C. Kelsey and Mr K. Hawkins.

The history of cricket in Braunton starts in 1875 when the village played a two innings match against Fremington, the score being Braunton 37 and 24, Fremington 21 and 24. In 1876 Braunton played another two innings match against Chaloner's School. This time the score was Braunton 50 and 55 and Chaloner's 30 and 78. These "two innings" matches went on except when playing against Georgeham on a new ground at Wrafton in 1878 just one innings was played as Georgeham didn't want to play anymore!

In 1880 the club was officially formed and matches were played against other local clubs. But by the early years of the twentieth century interest in the club and the game diminished. It wasn't until 1938 that it was reformed and has continued from that day to this.

A dedicated group of people raised funds by holding jumble sales, skittles matches and other

A few of the Braunton Cricket Club with the President Mr C. M. Kelsey who purchased the ground and gave it to the club. John Fry in the striped blazer.

The 1968/9 season. Back row L-R: Victor Lewis, Alan Sibley, Derek Sunderland, unknown, Wally Cockrell, unknown, unknown, unknown and David Shambrook. Front row: Don Newman, Ernie Shambrook, Capt. David Staddon, John Fry and unknown.

events. A tea hut and grass cutter were purchased and £7.10s was paid for the rent of a field off Moor Lane. There was then a succession of fields rented as a cricket ground from the Brittons, now a housing estate, then a field in Silver Street, followed by the war years at Chaloner's School playing field at Goodgates. The club is at home today in Field Lane and is called the Kelsey Ground.

Mr C. M. Kelsey, who lived at Saunton Court, was President of the club and when the cricket field came up for sale he knew it would be sold to a speculator who would build houses on it. He also knew the club's finances would not stretch to buying it.

Without discussing it with anyone he approached the vendors and purchased the field. When he received the final paperwork he went to see George Chugg at his newsagents in Caen Street. George, who was the club treasurer, was very busy with

customers at the time and so Mr Kelsey went behind the counter and quietly slipped the paperwork into George's overall pocket. It wasn't until the business of the day was over that George had the chance to look at the papers in his pocket.

There aren't many village cricket clubs that can boast that they own their own ground. The only stipulation to owning the land was that they would allow a hut to be built for the Boy Scouts. The Braunton Cricket Club field has been called the Kelsey Ground ever since.

A pavilion was first built on the field by the club members in 1939 at the cost of £29. A new pavilion was constructed and opened in 1967 at the cost of £1150.

The big event of the club's centenary year in 1980 was when they invited Somerset Cricket Club to play a match at Braunton. Test stars such as Ian Botham, Captain of England, and Viv Richards, Captain of the West Indies played and thrilled the large crowd of spectators. Braunton club has also had various Australian teams play on their ground as they always tour this country when their national team is in the U.K.

The club's top player joined the club in the colts section. He then went on to Braunton's first XI and then he joined Somerset C.C. Mark Lathwell eventually played for England.

John Fry, Mark Lathwell and Ernie Shambrook in 1992

President John Fry concludes that the club is going through a difficult time financially and they appreciate the support given them by the brewery and the trustees and while the club owns the playing area of the cricket field it is guaranteed that the game of cricket at Braunton is assured.

Braunton Bowling Club

The President of Braunton's first Bowling Club, Dr W. J. Harper, bowled the first wood on the four-rink green at Lower Park Road on the 26 June 1912.

Braunton's cricket team in their centenary year 1980. Third left front row is Capt. Brian Riddell from RAF Chivenor.

1980 Braunton Cricket Club v Somerset – the openers Popplewell and Wyatt make their way to the crease.

Centenary year – Ian Botham 'Out' (on the back of the photo it says) Braunton v Somerset, Appeals go up for 'Out'. Umpire Fry not impressed declares 'Not Out'! (Ian Botham is at the far end with his right arm in the air).

Braunton Bowling Club at Lower Park Road in the mid 1950s.

President Alfred Parkhouse bowls the first wood at the opening of Braunton's new Bowling Green at Chaloners Road in 1977.

Braunton Centenary Competition between Uffculme and Braunton, 29 June 2013. The Braunton players – back row on the far left: Barbara Poulter. Front row L-R: Les Court, Ken Capper, Phyliss Clegget, Sheila Court, Albert Yates, Peter Keyes (President), Mary Moule, Willie Bradford, Mike Poulter, David Staddon and Steve Vann.

The club was on the opposite side of the road to Tyspane Nursing Home, which in those days was a private house. The land was leased from Mr A. J. Tweedie and the four-rink green was prepared and made ready on meadow grass.

In the early days the matches were played under the 'Devon Rules' consisting of four teams playing each other on each of the four rinks for 11 ends, so the match consisted of 44 ends.

During WWI most sporting activity ceased in North Devon and it wasn't until 1920 that bowling recommenced at Lower Park Road club. In 1925 the owner of the land and President of the club presented a 'handsome' trophy, the 'Tweedie Cup', for the Club Singles Champion.

The members of the club had long wished to own their bowling green and in 1932 they purchased it from Mr Tweedie.

Thirty years later came the opportunity to move to a larger site. The Parish Council agreed to provide the land at the back of the Memorial Gardens on Chaloners Road and agreed to lay the green, but the club would have to maintain the site and build the clubhouse.

Work on the site began in 1963 and the club held a grand opening on the evening of 30 July 1966. Probably most of the conversation at the event was about how England didn't win the football 'World Cup' that afternoon!

In 1981 the Parish Council leased land beside the club which had been the Barnstaple to Ilfracombe railway line and so an additional two-rink green could be built. At the turn of the new millennium a purpose built clubhouse was opened. This provides all year bowling for members as it has an indoor short mat bowling facility.

Ladies have been involved with the Bowling Club from the earliest days but then it was only to provide the 'scrumptious' teas that the club became well known for. However, from the 1930s there were moves made to allow ladies to actually play bowls!

In 1967 the Ladies Section was formed and had considerable success in bowling for Devon County. I wonder if the men make the tea as well as the ladies!

Saunton Golf Club

Saunton Golf Club was formed in 1897, although it is thought that a golf course of some sort had already existed in Braunton Burrows for a few years. The first course was only nine holes which were extended to 12 by 1906 and to 18 holes two years later.

The course was re-designed by architect Herbert Fowler and opened in 1919 and gained a reputation as one of the finest links courses in the country.

In 1932 the British Ladies Championship was held there for the first time and members of the United States Curtis Cup team competed.

Once again Herbert Fowler was asked to design a new course which was completed in 1935 and became known as the West Course.

The Second World War saw the military take over the course and the clubhouse as the American Army used the whole area to prepare their troops for the part they were to play in the invasion of France. Tanks were parked in the dunes and over the golf course, causing a great deal of damage. With the hard work of the green staff and several prisoners of war the East Course was open for business by 1952.

The West Course was again re-designed and re-opened in 1974 and since then both courses have been updated with enlarged tees and new bunkers. Today, Saunton's two golf courses rank among the best in the golfing world with only one that has two better links courses, and that is the 'home of golf', St Andrew's.

Saunton Surf Life Saving Club

The North Devon Surf Life Saving Association was formed at Woolacombe after several fatal accidents in the sea. Brauntonian John Phillips, who lived at Woolacombe, became involved after a young holi-daymaker drowned who had been staying in his house.

John says it wasn't that the beaches were getting more dangerous but it was more to do with the great increase in the number of people visiting the area.

Chief Inspector Jack Tarr of the Devon Constabulary was a strong supporter of the idea and became the first chairman. He also allowed policemen to take part in practising and patrolling the beach during their duty hours. John Phillips became the association's secretary.

Although the club is mainly based on sport and competitions it maintains lifesaving aspects. It did regular patrols every Sunday from the 1980s during the summer but stopped in the early 2000s for insurance reasons. This problem was resolved and the club has a willing and well trained patrol on the beach providing free rescue cover for the public every Sunday and many Saturdays throughout the summer.

The club won 'Sports Club of the Year' trophy in 2001. This is the top national award for amateur clubs in Britain. Not only was it the most successful British Surf Life Saving Club in the competition but also supported the community, had a disabled group and a 'nipper' section. It had the highest points that had ever been recorded by the judging panel.

An inflatable rescue boat section helps provide safety cover on the beach and at national events such as the London Triathlon and has won both the National and European titles. Saunton Sands formed the first 'Flipper' section in the country for children under seven to learn safety and this has been copied by other clubs. The club supplies all this to the community for no charge (but donations are always welcome!).

With the co-operation of other Devon clubs a flood rescue unit is being developed, and would be on call nationally and even Europe-wide. This would be under the National Resilience Scheme.

Surf lifesaving, as an ethos or way of life, has come a long way in the past fifty years. The things that have not changed are the purposes, which are to save lives on the beaches and promote water safety.

North Devon Athletic Track

Albert Beer was a man of the soil. He loved his work in agriculture, working with the Ministry of Agriculture and then farming at Stoke Rivers for twenty-six years.

From school days he had many sporting interests, especially rugby and athletics. When he heard that I was writing a book about Braunton he wrote to me about his involvement with establishing North Devon's new athletics track. Sadly Albert died in 2013, a vibrant man who is much missed. His letter to me says:

In the late 1980s I chaired a public meeting at the Barnstaple Civic Centre. Forget politics, agriculture and the rest. This proved to be the most important meeting I have ever chaired. It sought public opinion on the building of a track to enable local athletes to enjoy similar facilities to those available at Plymouth and Exeter.

The idea was overwhelmingly supported and a development group was established to pursue the idea of a facility which now, over twenty years on, is worth a seven figure sum. Due to my heavy commitments with farming I was unable to chair the new development committee, but agreed to be vice-chairman. We were fortunate to be able to persuade George Squires, a well-known local sports personality, to accept the chair. The next question was location?

The project was well supported by North Devon District Council and the Devon County Council with an excellent site at Braunton Community College being selected for the new track. Local fund raising and sponsorship supplemented the finance contributed by official bodies. I recall a concert by Ilfracombe Male Voice Choir and Terence Higgins, then an M.P., sent a raffle prize.

Terence had, more than thirty years earlier in 1954, run the Bideford Bridge Race with Clayton Gibbs, Brian Kent Smith and 'Yours Truly' when Clayton equalled the clock at 8.00pm, the only time that the clock has been matched. Both Higgins and Gibbs were already international athletes and my old friend Brian Kent Smith ran for Britain in the 1960 Olympics.

The track was ready for use during winter 1989/90 and the official opening meeting was on 12

National Masters Surf Lifesaving Championships 2013. Middle of the rostrum the winner of the Beach Sprint – Ladies 40-44years, Georgina Martin. On the left the Welsh Champion, on the right 3rd place Catherine Chesworth. Courtesy of Andy Ford

Club Captain – Richard Follard of Saunton Sands SLSC with their beach vehicle. Courtesy of Andy Ford

National Championship Pool Lifesaving Manikin Tow Race. Courtesy of Andy Ford

Surf Lifesaving Great Britain Pool Championships 2012, held at Cardiff International Pool. In the front India Martin and next Millie Edge.

The clubhouse of Saunton Beach. Courtesy of Andy Ford

Billy Jo Ford in the Nipper Beach Sprint.

Catherine Chesworth in the Master Ladies Board Race.

Iain Bond in the Men's Masters in the Devon Championships.

Polly Pocock.

Masters Ladies Beach Flags. Courtesy of Andy Ford

Linford Christie at Barnstaple Leisure Centre looking at the plans for the athletics track to be built at Braunton. L-R: Albert Beer, Mike Saltmarsh, George Squires, Linford Christie, Ron Ruddan (Coach to Christie) and Freda Avant (Chair of North Devon District Council).

Nearly twenty years on from the first meeting Albert Beer watches his two granddaughters take part in competitions at the athletic track.

May, 1990. During the run-up to completion it was essential to maintain interest and one event was a visit by Linford Christie. Linford attended an event at the Barnstaple Leisure Centre which gained us useful publicity.

Now the track is well used and the envy of visiting clubs. An occasion of great pleasure for me was in 2008 when I saw my two granddaughters running on the track, competing for Dorchester Athletic Club in a League meeting which also included North Devon Athletic Club. A hard won facility but now a valuable asset.

Braunton and District Ladies Skittles League

Skittles has been a male dominated sport since the Ancient Egyptians founded it. Closely related to the outdoor game of bowls it is now usually played in skittle alleys in public houses. In Devon there is a well-supported skittles league which has six divisions and on average 15 teams in each division, with eight players in each team.

Braunton Ladies Skittles League was formed in 1961 by a group of women who were making a stand against 'men only' nights out. Once it was not the done thing for women to go into public houses unaccompanied. Many publicans refused to serve women who were on their own. And so this stand for 'women's rights' came to Braunton even before equal pay or the voting age dropped from twenty-one to eighteen.

The women set up their own team and arranged their own women's only nights out. In 1961 they began with eight teams and it rose at one time to as many as 40. Now there are 21 teams.

The ladies annual skittles dinner is one of the busiest days of the year for local hairdressers and unlike the men's dinner their partners can attend after 9pm.

Track and field events.

Held at the Agricultural Inn, Wrafton were the winners of Braunton Skittles League 1934.

Wrafton won again in 1937. Back row L-R: John Paul, Dudley Challacombe, Mr Harris, unknown, Alfred Harris, unknown. Front row: unknown, Tommy Joslin, S. Challacombe and the Skinner brothers.

First Ladies Skittles dinner held at the Parish Hall in 1962. The catering was done by Freda Prince at 3/6d a head. Freda had a café opposite Caen Street School. Ladies at the top table L-R: Joyce Mitchell, Diane Paddison, Audrey Newman, Lady Ruth Williams, Laura Ashton, Bette Crabbe and Margaret Foster.

The first ladies team that played at the London Inn were named the 'Rosebuds' and some of them met up again at the 50th Anniversary dinner. L-R: Shirley Lamprey, Jean Weller, Bette Hernaman, Doreen Shambrook, Phyllis and Dorrie Hicks who played for the Silver Bells at the New Inn in Church Street.

Chairman Elaine Christie cutting the 50th Anniversary cake.

A ladies skittles match played at the Mariners Arms on 23 January 2014 saw The Happy Wanders beat the Inn Things from the Agricultural Inn with Louise Roberts top score.

Chapter 15

Big Hearted Braunton

Twinning

Much thought was given when choosing the village of Plouescat in Brittany as Braunton's twin in 1975. Both villages are set in a rural area on or close to an estuary and on the coast with beaches. Plouescat is 12 miles from the French ferry port of Roscoff.

Founder and chairman of the twinning association was the headmaster of Braunton School and Community College Trevor Hickman. His aim was to create closer understanding and links with the French and to encourage exchange with local students and young people.

Both village communities exchange visits on alternate years, staying with local families and gaining knowledge and understanding of each other's way of life and practising the language.

The French arrange cultural visits and events to entertain their visitors and Brauntonians raise money all year with monthly social events to pay the expenses of their guests from Plouescat when they visit North Devon.

Both twinning groups compete for a challenge shield, a competition which the home villages organise and remain a secret until the day of the event. These fun days have included a tug of war, sack races, digging cockles, games of cricket and golf, fly fishing and sand castle building to name but a few.

When the Braunton Twinning Association visit Plouescat they usually take two or three students who practice the language and then give a speech at

The team of Braunton policemen who cycled to Plouescat in 1997. L-R: Sgt Roger Holmes, PC Phil Powell, a French policeman who called himself Charlie, PC Richard Bishop, PC Gary Osborne, PC Graham Lees and Sgt Keith Worthington and the lady President of the Plouescat Twinning Association Ernestine Miossec.

An early visit to Plouescat – John Incledon- kneeling front right.

The Braunton Twinning Morris Men and Women. Back row L-R: Phil Powell, Pat O'Hare, Ann Travers, a student, Hillary Clarke, Sue Thomas and John Rendle. Kneeling: Helen Forrester, Muriel Nixon, a student, Julia Powell, Sylvia Shilton and June Pratt.

a formal dinner. Braunton twinning has also provided hospitality for visiting French students with work experience.

Gifts have been exchanged between the two communities over the years. Braunton presented Plouescat with a Royal Mail post box and they reciprocated with a French postal service yellow letter box which is now in the side wall of Braunton Museum. Many more gifts are on display at the Parish Hall and the Braunton Academy.

Braunton Chairman Phil Powell and the French Chairman Patricia Choquer with the Challenge Shield.

EVENTS OVER THE LAST 100 YEARS

Charabanc Outings

Braunton National Deposit Outing, 12 July 1924.

A trip from Knowle to Cheddar Caves in 1928. Annie Chapple and Edmund Fry are the couple standing near the front of the vehicle.

Royal Occasions

Jubilee bonfire to celebrate King George V Silver Jubilee, 6 May 1935.

South Street residents celebrate V E Day, 8 May 1945.

South Street celebrates Queen Elizabeth II Coronation Day, 2 June 1953.

Coronation Day Carnival at Rectory Close, Wrafton. L-R: *unknown, Mrs Jarvis, Mrs J. Pace, Mrs Skinner, unknown, Mr E. Wood, Mr Jack Thatcher and Mr F. Skelton.* Knights Photographers

Wrafton continues to enjoy itself after the Coronation Carnival. Knights Photographers

Carnivals

1938 Carnival – William Easton as a Cossack on the horse on the left.

St Brannock's Young Fellowship dressed as characters from nursery rhymes in 1938.

In 1939 Nancy Lane and Betty Britton won first prize as Pierrot and Pierrette. They won a trip in flight in a Boyd's aeroplane from Chivenor aerodrome.

There were at least 20 floats in the last peacetime carnival in 1939. Dorothy Butler was the Queen that year and her parents who ran the bakery in Church Street watched the procession as it wound its way down to their shop – which is now Bakers Thatch – and then from another window they could watch as it reached the Georgeham Crossing before making its way back into the village. The Queen and attendants before the crowning. L-R: Miss Georgeham Tiny Brown, Miss Boucher as Miss Croyde, Mary the crown bearer, Queen Dorothy Butler, Miss Mackie representing West Down then Miss Marwood and Miss Saunton.

Mrs Incledon Webber crowns the Carnival Queen Dorothy Butler.

Tradition was broken in 1939 when they also had a Carnival King – Stan Squance arrived by train before taking his place next to the Queen's entourage.

The 1939 Carnival Queen is in the crowd at the first carnival after the war in 1947. Now Dorothy Baker, she is at the front of the photograph with the pram and her three young daughters, Geraldine, Pamela and Lesley

Kathleen Mitchell is the Dollar Baby and her sister Jillian a Hula girl and Daphne Meredith advertises Wills Woodbines in the 1948 carnival.

In August 1963 over 5000 people lining the streets of Braunton had the local newspaper declaring that this was the biggest carnival show of the century. There were 33 tableaux and 76 walking entrants. The newspaper reports says that the mile long route included the railway crossing in Caen Street, and the procession was broken up on the return journey to allow one train to go through to Ilfracombe. The Carnival Queen and attendants were chosen at a beauty contest during the interval at a dance held in the Parish Hall a few weeks before the carnival. This is not the 'done thing' today but in those days was quite acceptable. I have strong memories of this occasion as I was chosen as one of the Queen's attendants and remember being so nervous and quite embarrassed at having to parade around the stage while people marked their voting papers as to who they thought was the prettiest girl. However, I really enjoyed the carnival day when it arrived. But didn't enter into any more beauty contests! The Queen was Pamela Raby who was a dental receptionist and the attendant on the left of the picture was Peggy Brown who was working at a Saunton hotel, I was Avril Barthram from the New Inn at Muddiford and the two little girls were Jean Hookway and Jane Wearne and the crown-bearer was Julian Prowse. Courtesy Baths Photographic.

The 1977 carnival has a scarecrow competition. L-R: Ruth Byrom, unknown, Karen Demellweek, Steven Legge, George Legge and unknown.

The British Legion Brass Band play at the village fête in 1985. Some of the band members were Chris Passmore, Ossie Osborn, Dennis and Darryl Gibson, John Phillips and Eric Slade.

Showtime at the Parish Hall

We think this is the dance after the 1939 carnival as Peter Welch (5TH from the left in the middle row) has the same costume on as he had as the Carnival King's attendant in the afternoon. Can you spot anyone else you know?

Old time dancing in the hall.

L-R: *Mrs Jones and daughter Dawn, unknown, Jillian Mitchell and George Legge and unknown at one of the village dances in 1955.*

Braunton Productions of:

The Boyfriend *in 1978*

Hello Dolly *in 1984.*

The Braunton Theatre Group in Puss in Boots *in 1980.*

Tony Gale in Little Mary Sunshine *in 1977.*

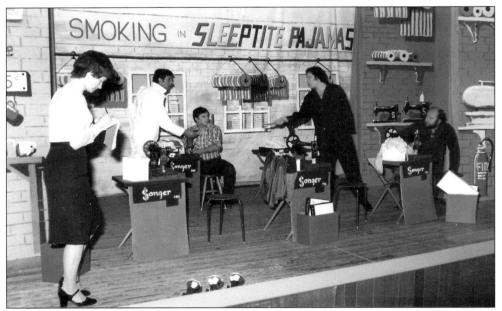

The Pyjama Game *in 1980. L-R: Lorna Greenslade, Tony Evans, Patrick Davies, Richard Haydon and Wally Stephens.*

Elaine Christie is presented with the Rotary Citizen of the Year Award of 2012 by Rotarians Stan Dibble and Brian Whiting.

Tug-O-War competition held every New Year's Day between the Agricultural Inn and the Black Horse Inn. Church Street outside the Black Horse is closed and the competition takes place in front of a crowd of up to a thousand spectators. The 2014 event raised £1800 to provide a defibrillator for the village.

The children want their go on the rope!

Welcome Home Parade as the Royal Marines from RMB Chivenor parade along Chaloners Road, 8 April 2009 after they return from service in Afghanistan.

Nick Harvey, North Devon's M.P. welcomes home 24 Commando Eng. Reg.

Storms and Tempest

Heavy rain brings floods to Braunton just before Christmas 2012 resulting in many homes and the streets of the village only fit for boats. Score Bridge cannot cope with the amount of water.

Local people spent many hours filling sandbags to try and combat the rising water.

The owners of Home Hardware in Caen Street do not lose their sense of humour.

After little more than a century when a great storm hit the coast around Crow Point, once again a night of storms hit the Westcountry and the sand dunes at Crow are washed away revealing the bones of a ship which had been covered for centuries by the dunes. The lighthouse no longer stands on the dunes but on rocks.

Margaret Clarke the eldest daughter of John Elliott the blacksmith in Church Street. She married seafarer John Clarke who owned the ketch the Democrat amongst others. Margaret's two brothers Herbert and William both gained their captains' certificates and her sister became Lady Nancy Young.

The Blacksmith's Daughter

During a terrible thunderstorm on 25 May in 1890, Margaret Elliott was born in a cottage in Church Street – 'a little premature', she told Lorraine Irwin, who recorded her memories.

Blacksmith John Elliott, was Margaret's father and her mother was the daughter of baker William Howard. Their cottage was at the bottom of Church Street and backed onto a stream that ran down from the hills. On the night of her birth the downstairs of the house was flooded. Out the back was a primitive toilet, a wash-house and a pigsty.

Everyone kept a pig in those days to be slaughtered when it was big enough. On the fateful day Shiner Mock would arrive with his wide belt with two or three big knives. The children had to stay indoors and watch all the comings and goings through the parlour window and the next time they saw the pig it was hung by its hind legs in the wash-house!

The meat had to be cleaned and salted for five days. Then the children would go round to the neighbours with a couple of pork steaks, chops or a bit of liver.

The stream when not in flood was a delight to Margaret and her younger brother Herbert and sister Nancy, and they would play for hours with jam jars

The bottom of Church Street in the early twentieth century.

147

catching 'Molly-heads' and 'crabs'.

When Margaret was three she started school and felt very important. When they came home in the afternoon the children would fetch water in pitchers from the pump at the top of Church Street. They had to fill a large crock to be used for cooking and drinking and this would take several journeys.

Another memory was of the lamp lighter who came round at dusk with his ladder and he'd light the wick in the street lamp. Next morning he'd be round again to turn off the light and polish the glass.

Another man the children envied was the Town Crier. He was very big and wore a fancy dress. He would walk round the village, 'crying' at the corner of the streets and finishing at the Cross Tree in the Square. Woe betide anyone who got in his bad books as he would, 'cry them up' and everyone would know what he meant.

The arrival of the London coach on a Saturday morning was always exciting. They would hear the horn a long way off and rush to the inside of the churchyard wall opposite the New Inn. The four horses would dash round the corner and the coach would sway and pull up to a halt. There would be people on top as well as in the coach and some would go inside the New Inn for a meal. They always seemed to be amused by the children and throw them pennies or half-pennies and then watch the scramble.

Before Margaret left school at twelve she says she had lots of adventures. Her mother's sister Nell lived in London and had a baby which died after a few months, "So I was sent up there, as a solace." She stayed for two or three years and went to school there. Margaret did not enjoy being with her Aunt Nell as she made her polish the silver and clean the boiler out after washing and do lots of other jobs!

Eventually came exciting news, Mr Gotto, the Vicar of Braunton would be calling to take her back home. It was the first time she travelled by train. Back in Braunton her mother was expecting another baby and she was needed to help in the home.

The baby arrived but he died. After a while another brother arrived and was named Bill after Grandfather William Howard. From the first time she held him he was Margaret's 'dear little fellow'.

About this time blacksmithing was taking a downturn and John Elliott decided to take on the licence of the Black Horse Inn which was across the road from their house in Church Street. So the family moved into the inn with its five or six bedrooms, tap room and cellars and a pump outside the back door – so no more fetching the water from the street pump!

Margaret says her mother worked hard in the pub, as the bar was open from 9am to 10pm and on Friday they were extra busy with all the farmers and people going through to Barnstaple Market and stopping in on the way back home. Her father would take over the bar duties and leave Margaret's mother to, "see to

things inside". (This meant all the housework and cooking for the following day.)

It was about this time that an act of parliament was passed that the school leaving age was raised to fourteen. The headmistress sent word to Mrs Elliott that if she wanted Margaret at home to work she could leave right away as she was a bright child and in a class above her age, if not she would have to stay at school for another two years. So Margaret left school and worked at home.

One day a man came to see how many beds they had to spare. The railway was having new rails laid and a lot of men were coming to work on it. They had six men stay with them and Margaret says it caused a great deal of work as they went off to work at 6.30am after having a cooked breakfast and with sandwiches or pasties for lunch. In the evenings they had a cooked dinner.

After this busy time was over Mrs Elliott thought Margaret should learn dressmaking and she was apprenticed to Miss Smith, a dressmaker in Caen Street. The business became so busy that they took on two other apprentices and it seemed a very happy period in Margaret's life. In fact she would go away on holiday with Miss Smith and they remained good friends all their lives.

With Margaret's brother Herbert gaining a scholarship to Chaloner's School and with his heart set on a career at sea and sister Nancy working at a florists in Ilfracombe, younger brother William was taken ill and had to remain in bed for several months. This left him with plenty of study time and he also heard the call of the sea. Eventually both brothers gained their Masters' Certificates and spent the rest of their working lives as captains of merchant ships sailing world-wide.

In 1910 the Black Horse was filled with workmen again when Horsey Bank collapsed in the Great Flood. Many of the men who came to repair the bank lodged at the Black Horse. As the work on the bank was governed by the tides the men would be working during the day and night. She says it was discouraging as everything they tried, failed to keep the sea from breaking through the bank they were building. Until at last a young man with fresh ideas sunk hundreds of iron bars, and hundreds of sacks filled with sand – which at last held and the tide was beaten!

It was also at about this time that Margaret met her husband John (Jack) Clarke. She says that at this time a scheme was raised to install engines into the little ships at Vellator to enable them to get over Bideford Bar safer and quicker.

One evening Jack came to the Black Horse with his brother George who was a regular customer, as well as being a fellow bell ringer and friend of Margaret's father. Margaret says they took a fancy to the place "and to us!" (that's Margaret and her sister Nancy) and they came to see the sisters whenever they were home from the sea.

Then one day Margaret's father took Jack Clarke to one side and asked him, "what his intentions were". Jack assured Mr. Elliott that they were honourable and that he would not be going north again but would only trade around the Welsh coast.

Margaret was taken to meet Jack's parents at Wrafton and two of his sisters who thought she was too young and didn't like it that she lived in a pub! However, things moved at a pace as Jack's sister Elizabeth was moving back from Simonsbath to Braunton with her husband James Welch who was taking charge of the new Braunton Electricity Company.

On 4 June, 1912 Jack and Margaret were married by Rev. Gotto at St Brannock's church. The bells were ringing and the church was decorated and full of people and Grandfather Howard made a huge wedding cake.

In the early afternoon they were pulled on a carriage by sailors to the station to catch the train to Mousehole in Cornwall for their honeymoon. After which they returned by sea to live in their new house, Bay View on East Hill.

Soon after this Nancy announced that she was marrying the young engineer who repaired Horsey Bank and they were leaving as he had a job to go to in Ireland. From there they moved to Shanghai for several years.

The following years brought happiness and sorrow in equal portions.

John Elliott gave up the Black Horse but kept on the blacksmiths while they moved into a cottage in Church Street.

In 1912 Jack's ship the *Edith* was mown down by a steamer off the coast of Lundy. The mate who was asleep down below was lost and Jack and the cabin boy were rescued after many hours in the sea.

There was great happiness when their first son Jack was born in July 1913 but this was followed by the outbreak of WWI when many little ships were commandeered by the Admiralty. Jack was stationed at Scapa Flow for six months at a time. This meant he only returned home twice a year for one week at a time – including two days travelling in each direction.

During this time their daughter Phyllis was born.

At the end of the war an epidemic of influenza swept through the country and one of its victims was Margaret's mother. It was a heart-breaking time for the family as Margaret's two brothers were away on long sea voyages and her sister Nancy was living in China. In the same year Margaret had another son who died at birth. But happiness was restored when baby son Frank arrived soon after.

The new doctor in the village Dr Traill realised that Margaret had been suffering a lifelong liver condition. He started her on a new treatment which stood her in good stead for the rest of her ninety-five years.

The Tailor's Son

To Brian Williams it will never be just another traffic light on the Square. He sees a tree; and in its leafy branches an owl.

"Before they widened the road and introduced traffic signals, Cross Tree stood in the Square," recalls Brian. "I used to listen to the resident owl hoot his nightly warning to the small nocturnal creatures in nearby farms."

His boyhood bedroom in the 1930s was above his father's outfitter's shop on the Square. At the turn of the century it had been his grandfather's 'Boot and Shoe Emporium'. Today it is an art centre.

For Brian the days began with the clip-clop of Farmer Hancock's carthorse as it was led from the fields to be harnessed for a day's work.

"Bill's whistle as he passed would be my signal to tumble out of bed, dress hurriedly and with milk jug in hand run up the street to the farm where Mrs. Hancock ladled the thick, warm milk from one of the great enamelled pans in the dairy."

On a September morn in 1935 he began his school days at Braunton Junior School in Caen Street. He was dressed in highly-polished laced shoes, knee-high socks and pristine grey shorts topped with grey pullover and tie. "My appearance bore witness that I was the son of the local tailor!"

His kindly teacher Miss Thorne kept 40 children happily content with plasticine, crayons and water paints. Favourite playtime games were cowboys and Indians and conker matches. And on Saturday afternoons they queued up for the children's matinee at the flea-pit (alias The Plaza Cinema).

On 24 May the school held its annual pageant celebrating the British Commonwealth. (The date had been Queen Victoria's birthday.) Children in costumes made by parents and teachers staged playlets about heroes like Captain Cook and Florence Nightingale and raised the rafters with 'Rule Britannia' and 'God Save the King'.

Favourite time of year, says Brian in his memoirs, was when the farmers harvested Braunton Great Field. "In early August we would travel out to the field in horse-drawn carts and watch the horse-drawn reapers cut swathes of oats, barley and wheat."

Rabbits, mice and rats would scatter to the four

The old Cross Tree that stood in the centre of the Square in Braunton.

winds, pursued by yelping dogs and yelling young-sters. The corn was then stacked to dry in stooks, "looking for all the world like Indian tepees."

A few weeks later it was piled high on horse-drawn carts with children perched on the top for the journey back to the village. "Surprisingly, no-one fell under the wheels of the cart or the hooves of the horses – but then, there were no health and safety requirements in those days so we didn't know what was expected of us!"

Vellator Quay was another popular haunt for youngsters when two-and-three masted coasters tied up from South Wales and Ireland. Skippers would recount their WWI adventures dodging enemy U-boats and E-boats.

On 11 September 1939 the simple, secure world of childhood was to change as a new war brought air raid shelters, sirens and blackouts to Braunton. The youngsters had to practice putting on gas masks ("we thought everyone looked like pigs") and a bomb shelter appeared in the school playground.

"Then Mr Richardson, our favourite teacher, left for service in the Middle East and a grave near Tobruk. The aircraft carrier HMS *Courageous* with a largely West Country crew became the first major naval casu-alty of the war and two girls in my class lost their fathers."

Evacuees from London arrived to be fostered by kind-hearted village families. "Once we accepted that most had never seen a live cow or lamb or been to the seaside, we got on quite well. It wasn't long before we were playing soccer for Arsenal instead of Plymouth or Exeter City."

Brian has a word to sum up his young days in Braunton – privileged. He adds: "Today the tractor has replaced the horse and combine harvesters have taken the romance out of harvesting. The sailing ships have long since disappeared. Dr Beeching put paid to the railway line from Barnstaple to Ilfracombe.

"I was fortunate to spend my early life in a North Devon village which was little changed from the time of my grandfather, and it left childhood for me as a heart-warming memory."

The Cross Tree is felled outside Brian Williams bedroom. No longer will he watch the owl as it sheltered within its branches.

The Moon Family

From his home on West Hill Ross Moon can survey the same vista that Sir Francis Drake is reputed to have said was the best view he'd seen in the whole of Europe. Ross can also look back over generations of his family in Braunton and most especially at his father's role in the village. Vivian Moon was born in 1922 at his parents' home at 11, Church Street.

In 1839 Ross's great-great-grandfather John Boyles Moon was born in Braunton and later married Lucy Watts and produced 12 children. One of these was Frederick Watts Moon who set up a bakery at West Cross at the bottom of North Street in 1895.

His two sons Leslie and Wilfred eventually took over the business, Wilfred continuing the bakery and Leslie concentrating on the grocery trade. In 1960 Wilfred took over the shop and Post Office at Knowle

Moon's Grocery Shop at 12, Church Street. On the right is John Watts Moon with his son Harold on the left and daughter Ethel in the doorway.

and Leslie enlarged the West Cross business and opened it as a delicatessen and café.

Another of John and Lucy's 12 offspring was Ross's great-grandfather John Watts Moon, who was born in 1866. As was his wife Caroline, and together they lived in Church Street where they ran grocery shops at numbers 10 and 12. It was here that their children Harold Morgan and Ethel Louise were born.

Harold – Ross Moon's grandfather, was born in 1896 and married Gertrude Eveline Johns from near

John Watts Moon and his wife Caroline Morgan Moon.

Gertrude Eveline Moon née Johns married Harold Moon and they had one child – Vivian Douglas Moon.

Vivian Moon. (He writes on the back of this photo, 'with my only two toys'.)

Vivian in his Chaloner's School uniform.

Aged eighteen before going into the Army in 1940.

1945 Rottenbeck Northern Germany with the 181ˢᵗ Field Royal Artillery.

Penzance and they had one son Vivian Douglas Moon born in 1922 at 11, Church Street.

Harold was in WWI but was too ill to go to the front so served his time as a farrier. Harold was a man of many trades, notably a haulier, as he had a horse and cart he would collect and deliver any commodity he could, especially coal. Harold was also well known as a turf accountant. In later life he went into the property business with several partners in a company called 'Bright and Gay'.

Vivian went to Chaloner's School and Ilfracombe Grammar but made an early start in his chosen career as an auctioneer when he joined John C. Webber & Son working part time, earning 14/- a week. He worked in their very first office which he described as, "just one room with only two chairs, one table and a door mat. However, the second office in Boutport Street, Barnstaple had three rooms."

On leaving school Vivian worked fulltime for Webbers and studied for his auctioneers exams. At nineteen he was called up for war service and joined the army. Following a distinguished war record he returned in 1946 and married Kathleen Mary Bull. Her grandfather Joseph Bull originally came from Barnstaple and Vivian had met his wife when she was visiting her family in the area.

Once back in Braunton with Kathleen (known always as Kay) Vivian took up his position again with John C. Webber.

Vivian started as an auctioneer selling chicken and livestock in Barnstaple Cattle Market. Vivian was an ambitious youngster and soon built up the business. Before long the estate agency was taking over from the auctioneering.

Vivian was given the chance to expand the business and soon there were Webbers Estate Agents in Braunton, Bideford, Bude, Ilfracombe, Lynton, Launceston, Taunton and Tiverton and by the early 1970s the company far exceeded anything that Vivian and his directors could have imagined.

When Charles Webber (son of the original owner) died the last connection with the name Webber was broken. However, Vivian kept his promise to his first employer and did not change the name of the business. And so Webber's to anyone in the West Country means Estate Agents.

Vivian Moon Philanthropist

Vivian Moon was very aware that he had come from ordinary village folk and his success as a businessman was through hard work (and probably a little guile) and as he got older he told his son Ross that he wanted to put back into Braunton what it had given him.

Vivian marries Kathleen Bull in 1946.

A Royal British Legion occasion in Braunton. L-R: Vivian Moon – President of the Royal British Legion in Braunton, Lt Col Of the Royal Marines at Chivenor, Derrick Spear – Chair of Braunton Parish Council, and 'Smudge' Smith Chair of Braunton Royal British Legion.

The village has benefitted from the Vivian Moon Community Centre, the Vivian Moon stand at the North Devon Athletics Track on Wrafton Road and the Vivian Moon Pathfinder Learning Centre.

Vivian also was a strong supporter of the Royal British Legion and served in every office in the Braunton Branch since it reformed in 1946.

In the late 1980s it was decided to sell Webber's Head Office at Deer Park to the North Devon Hospice for a fraction of the market price.

He also formed two charities – The Vivian Moon Braunton Community Trust Fund which helps fund the community centre, athletic stand and Pathfinder Centre and any group that comes within the jurisdiction of Braunton or Wrafton such as the museums in the village and Saunton Sands Surf Life Saving Club.

The other charity is a foundation which concentrates on further education for those between the ages of seventeen to sixty-five years. Ross Moon who is chairman of both these charities says that the foundation has awarded upwards of £400,000 in grants.

Ross Moon

Ross Moon was born in 1954 and by the time he was eighteen he was in London working in a Shipping Office trading in all kinds of commodities especially vegetable oils – mainly palm and soya oil.

By the age of twenty-one he had started his working around the world, Singapore, San Francisco, Switzerland and Malaysia where he spent twenty-five years and married his wife Swee Chin.

Ross returned to Braunton twenty-seven years ago and went into the property developing business and today he is semi-retired and feels lucky that he was able to buy the house his parents had built which overlooks Braunton's Great Field, the Marshes and far beyond. A view that so entranced Sir Francis Drake.

Ross, Vivian and Kay Moon. Courtesy Baths Photographic.

Bernard Watts

The story of Bernard Watts is entwined with that of Vivian Moon as for a while they were brought up together.

Born in 1912, Bernard didn't have the best start in life. Only a few years old he was found sleeping rough in a London park and although he had a family he was put into an orphanage.

Under a government plan to rehome children who had been left orphaned, by resettling them in the colonies, Bernard was given the choice of either Canada or somewhere in the English countryside. He chose not to go abroad and so in the early 1920s with a group of 40 other children Bernard found himself in Braunton.

The children were billeted in local homes or farms and brought up within these families. Bernard moved into the home of Mr and Mrs Harold Moon and their son Vivian at 8 Hillsview.

During his school life, Bernard told his daughter-in-law Christine, he had several part-time jobs such

Bernard Watts and Vivian Moon in the Moon's back garden.

as caddying for Sir Edwin Lutyens when he played golf at Saunton Golf Course. A much less pleasant job was helping out with Harold Moon's coal business by delivering coal to the hospital ship in the estuary by rowing out there in a dinghy.

In 1932 Bernard joined the Army and served in India for many years. In WWII Bernard won the Military Medal for bravery when in France he remained at his post with a large artillery gun and then blew it up as a German tank approached.

At Dunkirk he was blown up and so badly injured he was unable to continue fighting so he spent the rest of his war training other soldiers.

In peacetime and back in Braunton Bernard married Beryl Perks who worked at the Bulb Farm and then Cranch's Grocery shop in Church Street. They had two sons Bruce and Rodney. Bernard spent the rest of his working life at the 'Cotton Wool' factory – Kendalls at Wrafton.

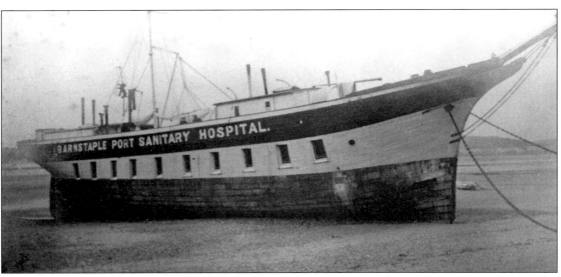

The hospital ship that was moored at Broadsands in the Taw Estuary.

Bernard Watts served for many years in India and whilst there was awarded the Royal Humane Certificate for saving a life.

Beryl and Bernard Watts with their son Bruce who served for many years in the RAF.

Subscribers

Ken Abbott (Jnr), formerly of 11 Station Road, Braunton

Marilyn Abbott, formerly of 11 Station Road, Braunton

Alison Ash (née Abbott), formerly of 11 Station Road, Braunton

Nancy Barnes, North Buckland, Georgeham

John and Mary Barnes, North Buckland, Georgeham

John and Gillian Barthram, Barnstaple

Denise Bennett (née Perryman)

Pat Birbeck, Wrafton, Braunton

Anthony Bond, 61 Moor Lea, Braunton

Willie Bradford, Braunton

Jenny Brannock Jones (née Sandercock), Hertfordshire

Michael Butcher, Leeming, West Australia (Braunton 1947-1961)

Cllr Caroline Chugg, Wysteria House, Willoway Lane, Braunton

Brian L. and Jean Clarke, Down Lane, Braunton, North Devon

David J.L. and Polly B. Clarke, Cannington, Somerset

Ian J.B., Patricia J. and Arron J.L. Clarke, Braunton, North Devon

Jean Clarke (née Incledon), Fleetwood, Lancs

Professor Jean Crabtree

Barbara and John Dadds, 1 Barton Lane Close, Braunton, Devon

Dot Davies, Braunton

Tracy Davies, Wales

John Davies, Wales

Paul Davies, Wales

Sandra Dickson, Seaton

Rita Iverna Buckler Drayton, Barnstaple

Julie and Jared Drayton and Sadie Iverna, Barnstaple

Anne Elliott, Braunton

A. J. Evans and J. Evans

David and Joy Fry, Barnstaple, Devon

Andrew and Jean Fry, Barnstaple, Devon

Janelle Gammon, Braunton

Andrew Henderson

George and Doris Hicks

Donald H. Hill, Station Road, Braunton

Victoria Hill

Joy Hill, Braunton

Margaret and Angus Horne, 'La Mer', Lobb, Braunton

Gill and Rob Hoskins, Braunton

Dave Hutcheon, Saunton Close, Braunton

Mike Inglis, Croyde, North Devon

Chris Irwin

Mr E. H. Jackson, School Master (Science), Braunton Secondary Modern (late 1940s)

Graham and Jean Jenkins, Homer Road, Braunton

K. Langley, West Park, Braunton

Pat and Ged Larkin

Gordon and Nancy Lewis, Cobham, Surrey

Paul and Ro Madgett, Braunton

Barnaby Madgett, Plymouth

Abbi Madgett, Ilfracombe

Andy, Georgina and India Martin, Braunton

Terry and Irene Matthews, High Bickington, Umberleigh

Stephanie Milburn (née Smith), formerly of 'Hills Court', North Down Road, Braunton

P. and S. Mitchell, Braunton

Ross Moon, Willoway Lane, Braunton, North Devon

Trevor Moon, North Street, Braunton 1937-1950

Graham Osborn, Grandson of 'Ossie' Osborn

David Osborn, Son of 'Ossie' Osborn

Pam Page, Barton Lane, Braunton

W. A. Patten, Pixie Lane, Braunton

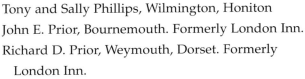

Tony and Sally Phillips, Wilmington, Honiton

John E. Prior, Bournemouth. Formerly London Inn.

Richard D. Prior, Weymouth, Dorset. Formerly
London Inn.

Douglas Reed, Newport Road, Barnstaple

Peter and Poppy Richards (née Woolway)

Elizabeth Ruckgaber, Berlin, Germany

Wendy Saunders, Willand Road, Braunton

Alison and Gary Serret, 43a South Street, Braunton,
Devon

Marguerite and Ray Shapland, Church Street,
Braunton

David Sharratt – Principal, Braunton Academy,
Braunton

Margaret Slee, 29 The Brittons, Braunton, Devon

Brian (Smudger) Smith, Braunton

Richard, Karen, Oliver and Jake Stone, Barnstaple

Ian and Sharon Stone and family, Milltown,
Barnstaple

Jamie and Tracey Stone and family, Barnstaple

Mr and Mrs Alfred James Tamlyn, Wrafton, North
Devon

Bob and Pat Thatcher, Barnstaple

David and Christine Thorp, Guildford

Jean Traill, Spain (ex-Braunton)

Norman Venner

Cheryl and Oliver Webber, Homer Road, Braunton

Brenda Whitney (née Sandercock), Cornwall

Ann Williams, Station Road, Braunton

Patrick Williams, Heanton, North Devon (born in
Braunton)

Brian C. Williams, Barnstaple

John and Dorothy Woolway

Brian and Angela Worth, Barnstaple

Geraldine Wright, Willoway Lane, Braunton, North
Devon